# Religious newcomers and the nation state

# Religious newcomers and the nation state

## Political culture and organized religion in France and the Netherlands

Erik Sengers & Thijl Sunier (eds.)

Eburon Delft
2010

This publication was made possible by a contribution from

The Van Coeverden Adriani Stichting

and

Zaich Taalservice

ISBN 978 90 5972 398 6

Eburon Academic Publishers
P.O Box 2867
2601 CW Delft
tel.: (0)15-2131484 / fax: (0)15-2146888
info@eburon.nl / www.eburon.nl

Cover design: Houdbaar Grafisch Ontwerp, Deventer

# Contents

# The national 'domestication' of religion in Europe

Thijl Sunier

The Islamic background of post-1945 immigrants to Europe has long been a minor political issue. For several decades, the religious background of these immigrants was taken as self evident and not very problematic. But the Iranian Revolution and its European offshoot, the Rushdie affair in 1989, and more recently the terrorist attacks on the Twin Towers in New York, the bomb explosions in London and Madrid, have heightened the sensitivity of policymakers, opinion leaders and citizens to the presence of Islam in Western Europe. Now, Muslims, or rather their religious traditions and values, are said to pose a new and unprecedented challenge to the national-religious status quo. There is a growing number of people in Western Europe that express deep worries about an, in their eyes, uncontrolled process of Islamization. They assume a continuous attempt by the 'Islamic world' to 'conquer the West' (see also Lewis, 2003).

Muslims and non-Muslims are living together in what are called secular liberal democracies. Muslims in Western Europe are exploring new ways of life and new ideas in a society where there is freedom of religion on the one hand, and an ever growing secularist militancy and national conformist pressure on the other. This controversy has largely shaped contemporary local, regional, national and global politics. What today is routinely called post-secular conditions are only to be understood against the backdrop of this dichotomy (e.g., Asad, 2003; De Vries, 2006).

Instead of assuming that this is a general clash between the secular and the religious, the modern versus the traditional, or worse insinuating that Muslims are here 'to take over', we approach the issue of religious newcomers in Western European nation states from a historical comparative perspective. The contributions to this volume may at first sight seem rather randomly chosen. They have, however, one crucial common characteristic: they address the ways in which Western-European nation states have dealt with existing and new religious diversities on its grounds and how these have been transformed into palpable social entities that are consistent with the requirements of national projects (see Casanova, 1994). Our cross-national and historical comparative approach and the long historical shot that we have taken demonstrates (1) that the roots of modern European nation-building lie way back in the early modern era, (2) that the history of nation-building in Europe cannot be taken as the history of the unilinear and inevitable retreat of religion from the public sphere, and (3) that the establishment of Islam in European societies has more parallels and similarities with previous episodes and other religious histories than is often assumed (see also Asad, 2003). Developments among Muslims in Europe illustrate this. They adopt ever more diverse ways of expressing and reproducing their religious convictions. Muslim identity is not anymore (or was it ever?) a simple matter of believing or not. New experiences produce new modes of religious identity and provide new sources of inspiration (see Vertovec, 2001; Cesari, 2004; De Koning, 2008; Ketner, 2008). This diversification of European Islam shows important analogies with the fragmentation of Christian and Jewish religious experiences in recent European history (McLeod & Ustorf, 2003).

Instead of treating the precarious position of Muslims in Western Europe primarily in terms of the internal dynamics of migration or to relate it to age-old stereotypes about Islam, we seek to analyze it primarily within the framework of the historical process of state formation, nation building and the evolution of civil cultures within Western Europe. The present enculturation of Muslims will be better understood, we believe, by comparing it with the way the European nations have coped with religious difference and the emergence of new religious actors now and in earlier periods of their history. The processes we refer to here can best be coined as the 'domestication' of religion (see Sunier, 2009; Al Azm, 2004). It is the process by which nation-states make religions fit for their national projects. Such a process produces particular political configurations and arrangements and it follows then that prior to the domestication religions are 'outsiders' or 'newcomers'. It is perhaps useful to keep in mind that religious newcomers do not have to be immigrants; they can also 'emerge' as a result of processes of religious reform or the transformation of the public sphere within the framework of nation building. Migration obviously adds an extra dimension, but it does not explain everything.

To analyze these processes this volume focuses on two contrasting cases: France and the Netherlands. Looking at the relation between church and state, the attitudes to cultural plurality and homogeneity, as well as at immigration and integration discourses, France and the Netherlands display both remarkable similarities and important differences. We seek to explain those similarities and differences historically, within the broader European framework. The hypothesis we put forward is that the specific historically grown characteristics of the process of nation building and the particular logics of the domestication of religious diversities are of crucial importance in understanding trajectories of religious integration. Thus the contributions show that the establishment of Islam in European societies has more parallels and similarities with previous episodes and other religious histories than is often assumed.

Three basic concepts essential to our approach should be introduced here: *religion*, *nation*, and *civil culture*. We argue that the nexus between these concepts provide us with a clue as to how the integration of religious newcomers evolves. To put it differently, neither specific characteristics of religious minorities, nor those of specific nation states alone account for the trajectories of religious integration and emancipation. It is the specific interplay between those two sets of characteristics that at once reflect and at the same time produce historically specific civil culture (see Baumann, 2004).

## Religion

Throughout human history religious difference has always been a source for both contention and interaction. One way to cope with religious diversity was pragmatism. As Michael Walzer has noted in his discussion of 'regimes of toleration', imperial governments usually promoted some variety of pragmatic, authoritarian tolerance (Walzer, 1997, pp. 14-19; see also Laursen (ed.), 1999). The Roman emperors, the last of the great pre-Christian empire builders, presided over a vast collection of local gods and cults. Religious syncretism, not homogeneity, was the rule.

Monotheism represented a new departure. Much more than its polytheist predecessors it was premised on a wholesale rejection of other cults as untrue and idolatrous (Assman, 2003). Drawing on Judaic and Greek sources, Christianity introduced a fundamentally novel view of the religious and its place in society. Its creative blending of universalism and exclusivity brought into being an expansive ideal of religious purity (Judaism, from which Christianity is an offshoot, is exclusivist but not aggressively universalistic). The religious other now assumed the hideous shape of a deadly infection of the social body. Admittedly, Christian regimes nowhere succeeded in eradicating all heterodoxy and folk magic - but it was not for want of trying. Both towards other religions and in dealing with internal dissent Christianity was a militant creed, perhaps unique in its insistence on a 'religious cleansing' of entire societies. Islam, world-historically closely related to Christianity, resembled it in this respect, although it was somewhat more tolerant of non-Muslim minorities in its midst. Recent studies on the early history of the expansion of Islam have shown that conquests were much less intolerant and violent than popular images would have it. Diplomacy was more common than among Christian conquerors (Kennedy, 2007; Lewis, 2008). Both Christianity and Islam are creeds of conquest and conversion, but the actual political practice was much more complicated than the creeds. They are, however, the two world religions that have spread most successfully beyond their places of origin. At the end of the twentieth century there were almost one billion Muslims and almost two billion Christians on a world population approaching six billion. In today's world Christianity and Islam are the only religions with a truly global reach.

The processes referred to here are about far more than doctrines and beliefs. They also, perhaps primarily, concern the definition and control of public space. Quite apart from their practical attitude towards 'non-believers', Christianity and Islam regarded all public space as their domain. Religion was not just seen as an attribute of individual persons but also as a property of social institutions. The conviction that religious homogeneity, or at the very least the institutionalized supremacy of the dominant religion, was a precondition of social and political stability common to Christianity and Islam. Christendom, like the Dar-al-Islam, was more than an aggregation of individual believers: both represented a social space organized by the visible landmarks and the organizational routines of religion.

Religion, then, was the foundation of civilization. The 'public' or 'state' church represented normality to most Europeans. Toleration turned on the question if other Christian churches, and in some cases the Jews, would be allowed to practice their cult unmolested. Likewise, there were limits to the public debate on religious matters, even in such relatively tolerant states as England, Prussia and the Dutch Republic. To the great majority of Europeans toleration and pluralism remained second-best solutions, while religious purity represented the ideal state of affairs. Muslims were generally of the same opinion: just as in England, Prussia and the Dutch Republic, the toleration policy of the Ottoman Empire was pragmatic and partial.

## Nation

Taking the nation-state as one of the central concepts in our analysis runs the risk of falling into the pit of methodological nationalism, the conceptual equation of society with nation-state (see Beck, 2000, 2002; Chernilo, 2006). The idea that the nation-state is the political entity par excellence of modernity and that the nation-state is the natural (even neutral) analytical level at which society has to be assessed, is still widespread despite its thorough critique in the past decades. Much along the line of the assumed naturalness of the nation-state, there is a widely held view that the spread of secularism as a political doctrine coincided with the emergence of the modern nation-state. The rationale behind this line of reasoning is that the nation is organized around the 'horizontal, direct-access character of modern society' (Asad, 2003). Asad clearly demonstrates that this is grounded on a particular notion of the modern state and its sources of legitimacy. The traditional state was based on force (in whatever form), the modern state is based on consent. With the emergence of the modern bourgeoisie there was no need any more to ground the state fabric in a religious transcendental, authoritative and compulsory doctrine. As a consequence religion and state gradually moved apart and became relatively independent spheres. This secular concept of the nation was grounded in the discourses of national law and national citizenship. A classical example of this idea of this horizontal access in conjunction with a civil consensus is the famous lecture of Ernest Renan delivered in 1882, *Qu'est-ce qu'une nation?* Renan at first deconstructs the concept of the nation, arguing that it does not rest on any objectively verifiable 'facts' of race, language, religion or geography, to arrive at the conclusion that the nation is "a daily plebiscite" which is ultimately based on the political will of a people to live together. He even asserts that the construction of a national past frequently rests on "historical errors" and the forgetting of "unpleasant" facts. Yet in the end he declares that the nation "is a soul, a spiritual principle", embodied in a collective memory and in the will to preserve and cherish the common legacy in the future (Renan, 1882/1992, p. 54). The idea that has been taken up by Renan and other contemporaries rested on the assumption that the plebiscite replaced as it were the religious imagination that the 'ancien regime' applied and that the nation-state as the natural political entity of modern society is not anymore based on transcendental imagination.

This is a gross misunderstanding. Asad has rightly argued that not only a secular sphere presupposes a concomitant concept of 'the religious', 'the political', 'the ethical', but also that governance in modern nation-states is not just based on either compulsion, or negotiation, "but on the statecraft that uses 'self discipline' and 'participation', 'law', and 'economy' as elements of a political strategy" (Asad, 2003, p. 3, p. 2, p.4). Imagined communities are always mediated through constructed images. These modern nation-state imaginations are as transcendental as religious regimes and secularism counts as the modern transcendent mediation.

One of the crucial mechanisms with which national imaginaries are constructed and made operational is history (Schiffauer & Sunier, 2004). The identity of a historical nation always presupposes definite historical memories, myths of ancestry, iconic symbols and rituals (see Connerton, 1989). And it was Bellah who introduced the term 'civil religion' to denote the quasi-religious language and symbolism modern (secular) nation states routinely employ to identify themselves (Bellah, 1966). Modern rituals of the nation do not fundamentally differ from religious rituals (see Salemink, 2009). As Alter (1996, p. 5) has put it: "In nationalism, the religious is secularized, and the national sanctified". To imagine a nation is to imagine the existence of 'insiders' and 'outsiders' even in those (rare) cases where the law is based on an impeccably inclusive conception of nationhood. In daily life as well as in politics most inhabitants of a nation routinely differentiate between the 'true nationals' those who 'really belong' and various categories of 'others' whose membership and allegiance are not so self-evident (see also Geschiere, 2009).

The social composition of nation-states, however, rarely corresponds to the nationalist dreams of purity. Religious diversity has always been a very crucial challenge in the making of modern nation-states as some of the contributions in this volume demonstrate. European states have confronted religions and churches in various ways, and this has led to diverging models of the relationship between state and church, and consequently between the national and the religious. In 'old' nation-states, such as France, England and the Netherlands, the process of nation building spanned the entire period from the Old Regime to the early twentieth century. In relatively young nations like Italy or Turkey this had to be accomplished in a much shorter time span. During the nineteenth century liberals, radicals and socialists sought to reduce the social and political power of the dominant churches, usually championing the separation of Church and State (Aston, 2002). As a result, national identity in post-Napoleonic continental Europe (the British case is somewhat different) tended to fracture into two competing national myths, one religious, and the other secular. The outcome of the conflicts over these matters largely determined the nature of the civil culture of a given nation as well as the place of the religious within it in the twentieth century.

Both the myth of national purity and homogeneity and the perceived religious diversity is part and parcel of the national imaginary. A crucial aspect of this imaginary thus is the question how to redress this perceived diversity. We call this process of the redressing of religious diversity the national 'domestication' of religion. This ties in both with what Asad calls statecraft and what Blom Hansen calls "languages of the stateness" (Blom Hansen & Steputat, 2001, p. 5). This brings us to the third central concept in our analysis: civil culture.

**Political culture, civic culture, civil culture**

Civil culture is loosely crafted upon the much older concept of 'political culture'. Political culture has been coined in the 1950s by the American political scientist Gabriel Almond, referring to a particular pattern of orientations to political action. A few years later, he further elaborated the concept in a comparative study on political stability, where they introduced the term 'civic culture' (Almond & Verba, 1963). The book became the standard work of the so-called 'political culture approach' in political science. Since then the term has continued to be a focus for research on political models and political practice (Formisano, 2001).

There are several reasons why we, however, prefer the concept of *civil* culture over civic culture. It first takes on board the relevance of civil society. It is basically through civil society, that "space of uncoerced human association" (Walzer, 1992, p. 89), that religious newcomers integrate into society. Formal civic rules that organize the relation between the individual citizen and the state can only partly explain how religious newcomers 'integrate' into society. The concept of civil culture takes up the normative and disciplining notions of how civil society and civil exchanges should be structured and conventionalized. An understanding of how civil society works is an essential ingredient in defining a nation's civil culture. Secondly, the concept of civil culture adds to civic culture the historically particular conventions in each nation-state about how a citizen should interact with the powers that dominate the public sphere, be they institutions of the state itself, judicial institutions or the rule of law, the conjunction of governmental and corporate powers, or plain civil servants running their bureaucracies. It connects the idea of civic culture, concerned with citizens vis-à-vis state bureaucracy, with the idea of civility. Thirdly the concept of civil culture takes on board the idea of a national imaginary as a crucial element in the trajectory to citizenship. Both civil society and civic culture unfold their dynamics in the presence of a state, notably a nation-state. The most effective means to turn a state cold and coercive into a nation-state warm and willed, lies in the creation of a national imaginary which imbues its organizational controls with a sense of identificatory community (Baumann, 2004). The wide variety of symbolic resources that contribute to this national imaginary can be considered as crucial elements in the making of citizens. Civil culture thus refers to 'political style', national values and norms, and modes and rituals of political decision-making, but also to collective memory, historical imagination, myths and hegemonic discourses. Civil culture thus allows for a rigorous distinction between society on the one hand and the nation-state as an active agent on the other. The variety of aspects clearly shows how difficult it is to pinpoint the concept to one definition. When we concentrate on issues of multiculturalism, citizenship and nation building, there are numerous comparative studies, mainly in the field of sociology, political science and political philosophy that refer to civil culture in one way or the other (e.g., Brubaker, 1992; Fetzer & Soper, 1996; Ireland, 1994; Schiffauer, 2004; Young, 1991).

Civil culture is thus one of the key concepts for comparative analysis. We start from the hypothesis that nation-states are active agents in the process of domestication of religion and that they indeed show differences in the way this process evolves. These processes are both the result and constitutive of civil culture. But having said this, we cannot possible assume that it is a thing unto itself. As we said before, the nation state as a unit of comparative analysis cannot simply be taken for granted. Against the background of the post-war influx of migrants from non-western backgrounds, the increase of transnational networks and processes of globalization, some scholars have argued that these developments seriously challenge the effectiveness of the nation-state as a powerful political entity and that we have entered an era of post-nationalism (for example: Soysal, 1994). Even multiculturalism as a political program, it is argued, seriously challenges the traditional nation-state concept. This explains why the nationalist backlash in many countries in Europe goes hand in hand with the demise of multiculturalist politics in the 21$^{st}$ century. Recent developments demonstrate that the nation-state still (or should we say again) plays a crucial role as a powerful unifying agent and repository of legitimization (see Modood & Werbner, 1997; Geschiere &Meyer, 1998; Favell, 2001). As a result of globalization and European integration and certainly since 9/11, European nation-states have recaptured terrain on the ever increasing process of transnationalism by reiterating and reformulating their historically evolved civil cultures. This implies that modes of civil incorporation, concepts of citizenship and models of integration differ considerably from one nation to another (Baumann, 1999; Schiffauer et al., 2004; Sunier, 2000). The acceleration of the process of European integration since the late 1980s (from the Maastricht Treaty to the Euro) has led to a growing awareness of national identity, and in some cases to a revival of nationalism and regionalism (Gingrich & Banks, 2006). It was because of the ratification of the Maastricht Treaty that France added a clause to its Constitution stipulating that French is the official language of the Republic. Globalization, economic crisis, mass migration and the spread of radical Islam has rendered nationalist discourse as the only viable answer to global anxieties.

We do not treat civil culture as a static category, but as the outcome of struggles that at the same time structure and shape further political processes. What a civil culture 'is' at a given moment in history is structuring and enabling for successive developments. Instead of assuming that every nation-state can be reduced to one single politico-cultural essence independent from time and space, we surmise that there is in every nation-state a historically grown set of peculiarities that can be identified as civil culture that takes different shapes within different contexts, and thus changes over time. Proper comparison can show us the working of a civil culture, but also its relativity and contingency rather than its presumed unchangeable essence. Thus when we take, for the sake of argument, the French notion of *laïcité*, the explicit separation of religion and state as an aspect of French civil culture since the early Third Republic, it does not mean that this principle appears in the same shape under all different circumstances. Aspects of this civil culture are contested and refurbished in the course of political contests. In this perspective, *laïcité* can be defined as a discursive field that is relevant to French civil culture in the nineteenth and twentieth century. A civil culture is thus an open-ended object of research, something that can be investigated empirically and comparatively. Here, we will focus on two aspects that are relevant for our discussion: in the first place, the national narrative that structures civil culture as a discursive field; and second, civil culture as a repertoire of memories, ideas, styles and rituals.

*Civil culture as national narrative*

A crucial element in civil cultures is the narrative about the nation, the national myth. As such it is a story of the nation about itself: the grand narrative about the national past, present and future. A further important aspect of national myths is that they are hegemonic. According to Haas, a national myth contains "the core of ideas and claims that most citizens accept about a nation state beyond their political divisions" (Haas, 1986, p. 78). Anderson (1983), Billig (1995) and others have argued that nation states articulate this myth through the creation of a national history. These national histories are of course contested, negotiated and rewritten over and over again, yet they shape dominant discourses, and their master narratives often possess a remarkable resilience.

History teaching and history textbooks are important sources for the analysis of national imaginaries. Moral communities are constructed by presenting the history of the collective to the next generation. In history textbooks a selection is made from the countless 'facts' and 'stories' that make up the nation's past, highlighting what is considered necessary to understand the present and omitting what is considered irrelevant. It is through history textbooks that the notion of 'what a nation stands for' is transmitted from one generation to the next. The concepts presented in history textbooks are, of course, not to be confused with 'reality': they reflect what the nation wants itself to be (or what it wants to be seen as), rather than what it actually is. As in every socialization process, children are not confronted with social life as it is but as it should be, sometimes in an almost self-stereotypical way. However, this does not mean that it is meaningless. On the contrary, principles of legitimacy are defined by transmitting who *should* belong to the nation, how a good citizen *should* behave, how civil society *should* function, who *should* participate and how solutions *should* be found (see Schiffauer & Sunier, 2004).

National myths and national narratives are of course also sources of conflict and contention. The present discussions about European unification, the controversies about national identity and in the general the continuous reinterpretation of the past, indicate the contested character of these hegemonic narratives.

*Political repertoires and contentious politics*
Civil culture not only refers to dominant discourses, but also to the political process itself. It can be considered as the argumentative repertoire, the storehouse of available political languages, gestures and styles that political actors have at their disposal. This repertoire has been produced in previous periods and previous political arenas. It structures subsequent political struggles and the outcome will set the stage for the next phase. In that sense civil culture conditions and enables. But at the same time civil culture is always in flux: it is a process. In the historical trajectory of nations we can distinguish between (long) periods of routine politics and (shorter) periods of contention, in which the basic parameters of a civil culture can be decisively altered. It follows that civil cultures frequently are transformed in relatively brief episodes of political conflict and thereafter persist over a longer time span of 'normal politics' (McAdam et al., 2001; Tilly, 1995).

A thorough understanding of the nexus between nation, religion and civil culture requires rigorous comparison. Each of the three parameters at stake has inherently essentializing characteristics when assessed in isolation. There are numerous studies that take religious affiliation and religious normativity as the point of departure for the analysis of processes of inclusion, assimilation and emancipation. Others take state formation as the decisive force.

We think that the dialectics between respective periods of contention constitute a useful starting point for our analysis of processes of nation-building and the reactions to religious newcomers. In the next part we will take a closer look at these fields of contention. Our working hypothesis is that the diverging reactions to Islam in different European nations are best explained by the different discourses of nationhood and the disparate civil cultures in those countries. If this hypothesis is correct, a historical and cross-national comparison of state formation and civil cultures, focusing on their incorporation of religions, will explain the differences and similarities between countries and in particular their responses to religious newcomers and their modes of making Muslim immigrants into citizens.

**France and the Netherlands**

Civil culture is thus both a discursive field in which certain narratives, values and exemplary events occupy center stage, conveying a script for 'correct' political behavior, rhetoric and style. Civil cultures in European nation-states are partly the result of political struggles over the relationship between church and state and the competing definitions of the nation in the nineteenth century. These were in turn inserted in a larger view of the origins and history of the nation from which certain 'lessons' could be distilled. The reason why we take France and the Netherlands for our comparison is that the history of these two nation-states shows both remarkable similarities and important differences. A brief comparison of the results of the school conflict in the French Third Republic and the Netherlands may illustrate this.

In France, where the Protestant alternative had been blocked since the seventeenth century, the school struggle was played out between Catholic clericalism and a secular-republican, 'Enlightenment' ideology of *laïcité*. The French liberals were thoroughly steeped in the art of mass politics and carried the majority of the nation with them. The conflict was especially bitter because it was linked to a more fundamental struggle over the nature of the political regime that had divided French society ever since the Revolution of 1789. After 1870, the Catholic party became deeply implicated in anti-regime politics such as legitimism and the anti-Dreyfusard movement. The very survival of the Third Republic was at stake. The separation of Church and State in the Combes laws of 1904-5 thus marked a double triumph: of *laïcité* over clericalism, and of the republic over its assorted enemies. As a result, the civil culture of the French Republic became a militant secularism that tended to exclude the religious from all of public space. This outcome enhanced the position of France's two religious minorities, the Protestants and the Jews, but not as religious communities. It was as individual citizens that Protestants and Jews were allowed to play an important role in the Republic.

In the Dutch case the school conflict evolved along different lines and the outcome was the reverse. Here, the *Ancien Régime* had not suppressed religious diversity but rather 'tolerated' and 'channeled' it under the tutelage of the political authorities and the Dutch Reformed Church. The liberal 1848 Constitution guaranteed freedom of religion, including religious schools, in the framework of the separation of Church and State. It was the attempt by the Liberals in the 1870s to impose a quasi-monopoly of the state schools that triggered fierce Calvinist and Catholic opposition.

As a matter of fact, the 'thoroughly Enlightened Nation' championed by the Dutch liberal leader Kappeyne in 1874 was not so far from Jules Ferry's ideas in France, tough it was somewhat less aggressively secularist. If Kappeyne's liberal offensive had prevailed the Dutch might have had their variety of the *État laïque*. But that was not to be. The Liberals had to concede victory to the confessional parties who proved to be far more adept at mass politics that the rather elitist Liberal gentlemen. A compromise was also facilitated by the fact that, unlike the French, the Dutch agreed on the political regime: the 1848 constitutional settlement was never for a moment called into question. The upshot was a system of organized diversity in which all religious groups enjoyed the status of 'minorities', even though a pervasive Protestant culture (but not any particular Protestant denomination) retained a dominant position. The outcome of the Church-State struggles shaped the party system and the political habitus of the French and Dutch elites. These were then inserted in dominant narratives of national history, which explained the success and vitality of the nation in terms of certain arrangements and virtues, which had proved their mettle 'over the centuries'.

National histories provide us with a central narrative around which national civil cultures are organized. Whereas the unity of the French nation is always threatened, the Dutch national narrative explains how diversity and national unity are successfully reconciled time and again. The 'great men' in Dutch history are not radical innovators but steadfast and earnest men who can bridge differences by means of skillful bargaining and moral leadership. In comparison with French history, rhetoric is less valued and negotiation more. Religious strife, erupting into civil war in the French story, is peacefully resolved by organized tolerance and mutual accommodation. In this view of national history, the pillarization model that emerged victorious out of the nineteenth-century conflicts between liberals, Calvinists and Catholics can be interpreted as a natural and typically Dutch development. Power sharing and the peaceful resolution of conflicts is the key to the prosperity and flourishing of the Dutch nation. Subcultures do not constitute a danger to national unity, so long as they play according to the Dutch rules of the game - that is the lesson of this history.

We do not wish to deny that there are also important common elements in the Dutch and French national narratives: for example, progress, toleration and human rights are core values in both cases. We are aware that the differences between French and Dutch civil culture should not be overstated. Since the late nineteenth century both are liberal polities in which individual rights are guaranteed by the constitution. But within the limits of the liberal model of politics and society the accepted manifestations of the religious in public space and the political representation of religious groups and their ideas have followed consistently different patterns. To sum up the similarities and differences between French and Dutch civil culture in a brief formula: French civil culture is liberal-republican while Dutch civil culture is liberal-communitarian. Or to put it differently: France may depict itself as a 'nation above (ethnic or religious) communities, while the Netherlands are a 'nation despite communities'. The dominant imaginations of nationhood have consequences for the perception of religious newcomers, whether they are immigrants or not. They have influenced the way Catholics and Jews have 'found their place' in the Netherlands, and Protestants and Jews in France in the nineteenth and twentieth centuries. And they are highly relevant to the cultural and political integration of Dutch and French Muslims in the contemporary period.

## Modes of inclusion and exclusion

A crucial aspect of any civil culture is the insider-outsider dialectic, the processes of inclusion and exclusion that are integral to nation building. Far from being a neutral legal and administrative framework, the nation-state is a socio-cultural network that produces an exclusivist discourse. The question of what is 'French' about France or 'Dutch' about the Netherlands can only be answered in terms of a particular, historical narrative. In such a narrative, some groups will occupy center stage while others will find themselves at the periphery. Likewise, some will be present in an early stage of the narrative while others will only make their appearance towards its end. In the course of the story of the nation, certain groups will move from the periphery towards the center, and the way that particular story is told is a defining characteristic of the nation.

Brubaker refers to citizenship as a form of social closure: defining who is in, means also defining who is out (Brubaker, 1995). Inclusion and exclusion can been studied as economic, political, legal, institutional phenomena, but also in terms of civil culture and the micro-sociology of daily life. Every national civil culture has its own historically grounded notions of who belongs to the nation and who does not, and how one becomes a member of a nation. This is often referred to as 'integration', or 'civic incorporation'. In his study of civil culture Schiffauer (1997) analyzes the different modes of civic incorporation in four European nation-states and shows how similar processes work out differently in the context of different civil cultures. Consequently, every nation-state defines 'integration' in a different way.

Many contemporary debates about integration tend to be confused because people assume that integration means basically the same thing regardless of the context. Thus in some cases integration equals assimilation, but in others it does not. For example, the French ideal notion of citizenship is inclusive in that it makes no distinction on the basis of race, religion or culture, but at the same time it is exclusive because it rules out every reference to religious or ethnic peculiarities. The French 'nation above communities' idea is: play the French card, and use the options offered by the French civil project. The ethnic and religious cards are taboo because they do not fit into the French republican ideology (Jansen, 2006). In France, it is a legitimate argument to accuse someone of 'communitarian' practices that run counter to republican universalism. The French state does not formally recognize 'minorities'.

In the Dutch case integration carries a different message, although Dutch civil culture had assimilationist underpinnings from the early 1980s onwards, there is a difference in the way this is achieved. In the 1980s and much of the 1990s the legal and institutional fabric of the Dutch system left plenty of room for religious newcomers to set up their own institutions. 'Minorities' were politically recognized, religious liberty was traditionally interpreted in a broad manner, and the Constitution guarantees all religious groups the right to found their own schools, funded by the state. These 'multicultural' policies are easily grafted on the national myth of Dutch tolerance towards Jews and other 'minorities' that can be traced back to the seventeenth century. At the same time there is a strong emphasis on participation in the Dutch moral community where all 'minorities' are called upon to 'overcome' their differences. Thus in the Dutch case one has to apply a different strategy when it comes to effective argumentation and negotiation. One may emphasize ethnic or religious background as an important part of one's identity, as long as it does not lead to separation from the larger 'national community'. The ethnic card is acceptable, but it is always seen as second best and principally temporal. Members of minorities are encouraged to look for similarities with the dominant population rather than differences. Inclusive argumentative strategies are favored above exclusivist ones. In short, the image that the Netherlands is multiculturalist is seriously misleading because it assumes that 'the recognition of ethnic and religious diversity' constitutes a binding principle of civil culture. Such a recognition, however, has never existed (Sunier, 2010).

It is important to notice that in most cases, insider-outsider configurations are not simple dichotomies. We must rather picture a nation as a series of concentric circles: located at the center of nation X are those who represent the very essence of 'X-ness'. Towards the outer circles perceived cultural distance from the center increases. All nationals are equal but some are more equal than others and this changes over time. Time and collective memory are of great significance in the outsider-insider dialectic. Over time, the perceived 'otherness' of old newcomers decreases, while the 'otherness' of the most recent newcomers is often represented in essentialist terms: there frequently is a strong tendency to ascribe all their 'problems' to their religious identity, a sort of Weberian Protestant-ethic thesis in reverse (and historically just as implausible).

Seen in this context, national integration has not, in fact, brought about the homogenization of culture nineteenth-century nationalists dreamed about, but rather a progressive 'domestication', 'softening' and 'forgetting' of once all-important. However, the transition from X-believers who are also Z-nationals to Z-nationals who are also X-believers is a long and painful one, which frequently goes on long after it seems to be over. A good example is anti-Semitism. After the Holocaust, the Western world adopted the inclusive notion of a Judeo-Christian civilization, while before 1940, many, perhaps the majority, were inclined to envision the relation between Jewish and Christian culture in terms of a 'clash of civilizations'. After the defeat of Nazi Germany the Jews were accepted as fellow nationals who had once and for all shed their erstwhile 'otherness'. And although not everybody may embrace this post-war inclusive consensus, there seems to be an implicit and sometimes very explicit resistance against the idea that some time in future we may refer to the 'Judeo-Christian-Islamic' foundations of European civilization.

It should be emphasized that we do not intended to draw as it were the whole picture in both France and the Netherlands. This would not only be a gross overstatement of our ambitions, it would also largely neglect the complexities of processes of nation-building. Our main hypothesis is that nation-states are never accomplished. Religious newcomers step into an existing political realm, but by doing so, they are already altering the existing status quo (cf. Asad, 2003). What we however intend to do in this volume is to present the outlines of a politico-historical comparative methodology to come to grips with *contemporary* relations between nation-states and religious newcomers/religious diversity. Such a methodology should necessarily present itself not as a closed theoretical argument but rather as an ongoing academic debate. The chapters in this volume must thus be considered as contributions to that debate.

## Outline of the book

The authors to this volume have taken up the broad outline sketched in this introduction. Each of the contributions takes the complex relations between (nation-) state building and religious presence as the starting point for their argument. The book is divided in two parts. In the first part, some general remarks about religion and nation-state, in historical and political perspective, are made. Te Brake in a European and comparative perspective, Van Rooden and Massignon trace the origins of civil culture in the Netherlands and France respectively. In the second part, four case-studies on religious newcomers in France and the Netherlands are presented: Catholics in the Netherlands (Sengers), Protestantism in France (Willaime), Islam in the Netherlands (Sunier) and Islam in France (Maussen). The volume is closed by concluding remarks of James Kennedy.

The Brake opens with a number of very crucial observations. First, exploring religious wars and inter-religious cohabitation in early modern Europe requires us to focus on the often unintended consequences of the historical *interaction* of authoritative claims/discourses and challenging or dissenting counterclaims, not just one or the other. Secondly, these insights force us to abandon the dominant dichotomy traditional/modern when it concerns the issue of the accommodation of religious diversity and to acknowledge that the idea of universal human rights as the decisive marker of modernity is utterly questionable. As the Brake argues, long term historical analysis provide us with the opportunity to discover the recurrent processes that make for peaceful religious coexistence in the context of polarization, violence and even war throughout history. Te Brake then arrives at the conclusion that "perhaps the most enduring obstacle to understanding the on-going historical process of accommodating religious and cultural differences is the academic myth that national state formation and democratization wiped the ‘traditional’ slate clean and set the stage for unprecedented challenges, like multiculturalism, in a fundamentally ‘modern’ world”.

Van Rooden, in dealing with religious diversity and state formation in the Netherlands, arrives at a somewhat different conclusion and argues that we have to acknowledge the huge shifts that have taken place in the way the Netherlands have dealt with religious diversity over the past centuries. Although religion has always been the main boundary marker in the process of state formation in the Netherlands, the actual make-up of these processes show tremendous differences over time. Van Rooden proposes a radical distinction between the ‘ancien regime’ and the era following the emergence of the modern secular nation-state.

In treating the French concept of *laïcité*, Massignon argues that we should be very cautious not to imbue the concept of political culture (or civil culture for that matter) with too much explanatory power. She proposes a much more interactive approach to the concept by treating political culture from a more semiotic, interpretive angle. She clearly demonstrates how *laïcité* to a large extent depends on the specific context in which it is applied. Rather than an explanatory political principle, it functions as a contextual narrative that legitimizes and delegitimizes political decision making.

The second part of the book opens with the contribution of Erik Sengers on Dutch Catholicism. Catholicism was not a religious newcomer in the strict sense, he states, as this religion has been present since the early Middle Ages. Moreover, as the constitutional framework has been relatively constant since the nineteenth century, the question is not how the state reacted to this newcomer. The question Sengers deals with is how Catholics vehemently tried to become accepted, ordinary citizens in a predominantly Protestant socio-cultural framework, a framework that gradually lost power not the least through the attacks of Catholics and neo-Calvinists. He shows how Catholicism in its opposition to the modern state gradually adapted to that same state, and how the state through funding and broadening its national conception managed to accommodate Catholicism. In the end, Catholics and their church no longer were the ‘others’ but were seen as (and saw themselves) as an accepted denomination.

A different trajectory is that of Protestantism in France. Whereas Catholics in the Netherlands adapted to the general culture, Willaime describes in his contribution how the overwhelming but declining position of Catholicism ànd the influx of protestants from immigration countries has led to an increase of protestant identity and visibility in the country once characterized as 'the mother of the [Catholic] Church'. Despite its minority position, Protestantism has contributed considerably and in various ways to French nation and society: in social and cultural works, and in taking the lead in ecumenical contacts. At the same time, the discussions about sexual ethics (homosexuality and recognition of non-marital relationships) and the development of political values among protestants (from left-wing to right-wing) have on the one hand brought Protestantism closer to the general culture, on the other hand have split Protestantism into more liberal and more orthodox groups. The future of French Protestantism will develop in the socio-cultural framework of the French society as a whole that can be interpreted as a 'protestantization' of France: growing individualism and de-institutionalization that affects every religious organization, and increasing influence of capitalist values. But most important: the picture of France as a Catholic nation is changing rapidly and Protestant groups have to find a way to remain a visible and viable position in this new field.

In discussing the ways in which the Netherlands have dealt with Islam over the past decades, Sunier argues that neither short term analysis of political governance, nor long term political principles alone can account for the particular characteristics of Dutch civil culture. It is the outcome of specific contentious episodes conditioned by the nexus between formal legal arrangements, short term political decision making and shifting national imaginaries that reach back to the early days of the modern Dutch nation-state that make up civil culture. The past is actively staked to take positions in the political process. In these contentious episodes key concepts such as tolerance, secularism, multiculturalism and national identity take different shapes and have different implications.

In his treatment of the delicate balance in France between fundamental republican principles and the undeniable fact that Muslims articulate demands as a religious community, Maussen shows how the concept of laïcité as a vexed point of reference is constantly reproduced under changing circumstances. Recent developments have rendered Islam a status of urgency. He ends up with three crucial issues that continue to frame the discussion on Islam in France. The first concerns the interaction of the state with Muslim organizations. Governments are in need of interlocutors, regardless of the separation between church and state, of organizations that qualify as representatives of the 'Muslim population'. The second issue concerns the relation between the principle of equal treatment of Islam as a minority religion, and the protection of effective religious freedom of Muslims. This relation is far from unambiguous. The third issue concerns the citizenship status of Muslims. French policy is based on the notion that citizenship and *laïcité* mean that Muslims in France have the opportunity to demand their rights as citizens. Much as the second issue, this leaves French politics with an 'unsolved' dilemma. In a final chapter Kennedy brings together the contributions to this volume and draws some general conclusions.

## References


Al-Azm, S. (2004). *Islam, terrorism and the West today*. Amsterdam: Praemium Erasmianum Foundation.

Almond, G.A. & Verba, S. (eds.) (1963). *The civic culture: Political attitudes and democracy in five nations*. Princeton, NJ: Princeton University Press.

Alter, P. (1996). *Nationalism*. London: Arnold.

Asad, T. (2003). *Formations of the secular: Christianity, Islam, modernity*. Stanford: Stanford University Press.

Assman, J. (2003). *Die mosaische Unterscheidung*. München-Wien: Carl Hanser Verlag.

Aston, N. (2002). *Christianity and revolutionary Europe 1750-1830*. Cambridge: Cambridge University Press.

Baumann, G. (1999). *The multicultural riddle*. London: Routledge.

Baumann, G. (2004). Introduction: Nation-state, schools and civil enculturation. In W. Schiffauer, G. Baumann, R. Kastoryano & S. Vertovec (eds.), *Civil enculturation: Nation-state, school and ethnic difference in four European countries* (pp. 1-18). Oxford: Berghahn Publishers.

Beck, U. (2000). *What is globalization?* Cambridge: Polity Press.

Beck, U. (2002). The cosmopolitan society and its enemies. *Theory, culture & society,19*(1–2), 17–44.

Bellah, R. (1967). Civil religion in America. *Daedalus,* 96 1-21.

Blom Hansen, T. & Stepputat, F. (eds.) (2001). *States of imagination: Ethnographic explorations of the postcolonial state.* London: Duke University Press.

Brubaker, R. (1992). *Citizenship and nationhood in France and*

*Germany*. Cambridge: Harvard University Press.
Cesari, J. (2004). *L'Islam à l'épreuve de l'Occident*. Paris: La Découverte.
Chernilo, D. (2006). Social theory's methodological nationalism. *European Journal of Social Theory, 9*(1), 5-22.
Connerton, P. (1989). *How societies rember*. Cambridge: Cambridge University Press.
De Koning, M. (2008). *Zoeken naar een 'zuivere' islam: Geloofsbeleving en identiteitsvorming van jonge Marokkaans Nederlandse moslims*. Amsterdam: Bert Bakker.
De Vries, H. (2006). *Political theologies: Public religions in a post-secular world*. New York: Fordham University Press.
Favell, A. (2001). *Philosophies of integration: Immigration and the idea of citizenship in France and Britain*. New York: Palgrave.
Fetzer, J.S. & Soper, J.C. (2005). *Muslims and the state in Britain, France and Germany*. Cambridge: Cambridge University Press.
Formisano, R.P. (2001). The concept of political culture. *Journal of interdisciplinary history, 31*(3), 393-426.
Geschiere, P. (2009). *Perils of belonging: Autochthony, citizenship and exclusion in Africa and Europe*. Chicago: University of Chicago Press.
Geschiere, P. & Meyer, B. (1998). Globalization and identity: Dialectics of flow and closure. *Development and Change, 29*(4), 601-615.
Gingrich, A. & Banks, M. (eds.). (2006). *Neo-nationalism in Europe and beyond*. Oxford: Berghahn.
Ireland, P. (1994). *The policy challenge of ethnic diversity*. Cambridge: Harvard University Press.
Jansen, Y. (2006). *Stuck in a revolving door: Secularism, assimilation and democratic pluralism*. PhD-thesis University of Amsterdam.
Kennedy, H.N. (2007). *The great Arab conquests: How the spread of Islam changed the world we live in*. London: Weidenfeld&Nicolson.
Ketner, S. (2008). *Marokkaanse wortels, Nederlandse grond: Exploratie, bindingen en identiteitsstrategieën van jongeren van Marokkaanse afkomst*. PhD Rijksuniversiteit Groningen.
Laursen, J.C. (ed.). (1999). *Religious toleration: The variety of rites from Cyrus to Defoe*. Basingstoke & London: MacMillan.
McLeod, H. & Ustorf, W. (eds.). (2003). *The decline of Christendom in Western Europe 1750-2000*. Cambridge: Cambridge University Press.
Lewis, B. (2003). *What went wrong? The clash between Islam and*

*modernity in the Middle East.* New York: Perennial.
Lewis, D.L. (2008). *God's crucible: Islam and the making of Europe 570 to 1215.* New York: Norton.
McAdam, D., Tarrow, S. & Tilly, C. (2001). *Dynamics of contention.* Cambridge: Cambridge University Press.
Modood, T. & Werbner, P. (eds.). (1997). *The politics of multiculturalism in the New Europe.* London: Zed Books.
Renan, E. (1992). *Qu'est-ce qu'une nation? et autres essais politiques.* Paris: Presses Pocket. (original work published 1882).
Salemink, O. (2009). Nederland H-6 land? Rituele definities van de natie. In T. Sunier (ed.), *Antropologie in een zee van verhalen* (pp. 137-167). Amsterdam: Aksant.
Schiffauer, W. & Sunier, T. (2004). Representing the nation in history textbooks. In W. Schiffauer, G. Baumann, R. Kastoryano & S. Vertovec (eds.), *Civil enculturation: Nation-state, school and ethnic difference in four European countries* (pp. 33-60). Oxford: Berghahn Publishers.
Soysal, Y.N. (1994). *Limits of citizenship: Migrants and postnational membership in Europe.* Chicago: University of Chicago Press.
Sunier, T. (2000). Civil enculturation: Nation-state, school and ethnic difference in four European countries. *Journal of international migration and integration, 1*(3), 305-330.
Sunier, T. (2009). *Beyond the domestication of Islam in Europe* Amsterdam: VU University (inaugural lecture).
Sunier, T. (2010). Assimilation by conviction or coercion? Integration Policies in the Netherlands. In A. Silj (ed.), *European multiculturalism revisited.* London: Zed Books.
Tilly, C. (1995) Citizenship, identity and social history. *International Review of Social History, 40*(3), 1-18.
Vertovec, S. (2001). Moslimjongeren in Europa: Vermenging van invloeden en betekenissen. In D. Douwes (ed.), *Naar een Europese Islam?* (pp. 95-117). Amsterdam: Mets & Schilt.
Walzer, M. (1997). *On toleration.* New Haven-London: Yale University Press. Young, I. M. (1990). *Justice and the politics of difference.* Princeton, NJ: Princeton University Press.

# Part 1: origins and importance of political cultures

# Accommodating difference

## Historical processes and political cultures

Wayne te Brake

### Introduction

The agenda for comparative research on the problem of 'Explaining the reactions of nations to religious newcomers' is a very ambitious and promising one. Highlighting critical differences in the national histories of France and the Netherlands challenges us to think anew about critical contemporary issues – like the variable meaning of political integration for religious 'outsiders', the deeply contested religious agency of women, and the distressing logic of cultural misunderstanding – that have deep historical roots. I would like in this essay to ask what we might learn if we expand the historical dimension of the explanatory problem – if we look back beyond the period when churches were formally separated from states. In the end, I should like to suggest that political cultures are more clearly the *explicandum* – that is, complex sets of shared understandings about politics and political participation that need to be explained historically – than the principal factor to explain distinctive histories. But first, we will need to enter into the often bitter religious conflicts and wars that characterized Reformation and post-Reformation Europe. For Europe's infamous 'Age of Religious Wars' produced simultaneously, if somewhat paradoxically, both religious intolerance and religious coexistence and, in the process, gave birth to the political-cultural variations of modern Europe that structure the integration of religious newcomers.

### The politics of religious war

Though I would like to focus on the cultural politics of the religious peace that ensued, we should begin with a quick look at the reality of the religious wars. The table, which lists only the most prominent of the wars in summary fashion, is at once familiar and depressing: in fact, the German Peasants' War, the French Civil Wars, The Thirty Years' War, and Cromwell's military campaign in Ireland are among the most destructive in European history prior to the twentieth century. And while the bulk of the fighting took place north of the Alps and Pyrenees, virtually all of Europe, including Iberia, Italy, and Scandinavia, were involved in the prosecution of these wars. What made these wars *religious*, it seems to me, is a combination of three things:

1. In each of them (with the possible exception of the Peasants' War) religious identities served as a primary marker of political difference and opposition;
2. The combatants were supported by larger networks of trust based on religious affiliations and solidarities;
3. The outcomes of these conflicts had significant consequences for the political relationships of the religious groups that were engaged in the struggle (compare the more restrictive version of these criteria in Te Brake, 1998, p. 115).

Table: Religious wars in Early Modern Europe

| **Religious war** | **Place** | **Time period** | **Military outcome or peace settlement** |
|---|---|---|---|
| Peasants' War | Germany Switzerland | 1524-1526 | No settlement; local capitulations of rebel armies |
| Kappel Wars | Switzerland | 1529-1531 | Peace of Kappel (1529, 1531) |
| Schmalkaldic Wars | Germany | 1545-1555 intermittently | Peace of Augsburg (1555) |
| Civil/ Religious Wars | France | 1562-1627 intermittently | Separate Edicts ended each of the nine wars; most successful Edict of Nantes (1598), revoked by Louis XIV (1685) |
| Eighty Years' War | Low Countries | 1568-1648 | Pacification of Ghent (1576), Twelve Years' Truce (1609-1621), and Treaty of Münster (1648) |
| Thirty Years' War | Germany | 1618-48 | Peace of Westphalia (1648) |
| Civil Wars | Scotland Ireland England | 1638-51 | End in England with execution Charles I (1649); end in Ireland & Scotland with Cromwell's military campaigns (1650-51); monarchy restored 1660 |

Highlighting these relational criteria – as opposed to cognitive criteria revolving around individual motives and intentions – is important because it helps us to identify the recurrent processes that led from religious controversy to war and, by extension, from armed struggle to relatively peaceful coexistence.

In the early sixteenth century, the so-called 'Luther question' served mightily to divide European Christians into multiple religious camps, with diminishing space as time went on for neutrality among them (Cameron, 1991; Tracy, 1999). Though the specific identities remained fluid for some time and their labels varied from place to place, the most common thread was a basic division between those who attacked the theology and ritual practices of the established Latin Church, with its ecclesiastical centre in Rome, and those who defended the orthodoxy and unity that Rome claimed to represent. The nascent religious identities that divided the critics from the defenders became *politicized* when civil authorities, often reluctantly, chose one side or the other in the growing struggle, and groups of their subjects *mobilized* collectively to support one side or the other. In this way, religious identities like 'Lutheran', 'Calvinist', 'Anabaptist', 'Roman', 'Papist', 'orthodox', 'heretic' or 'dissenter' became potentially important markers simultaneously of religious oppositions and political differences. In this explosive context, then, local conflicts recurrently *activated* some specific variation of the reform/counter-reform identity boundary, and when third parties, especially broader networks of trust based on identification with one or the other of these increasingly polarized choices, acted to support the local combatants, these conflicts *escalated* to become categorical fights invoking some version of the general reform/counter-reform identity boundary. What happened in addition in each of the cases I have listed is that political entrepreneurs brokered larger coalitions and alliances that prominently *incorporated* specialists in coercion, like the captains of militias or the commanders of armies. In short, I believe that politicization, mobilization, activation, escalation and incorporation are recurrent processes that can be identified in the run-up to each of the religious wars.

Even a quick review of the list of religious wars suggests, however, that these recurrent processes did not mechanically produce invariant outcomes. On the contrary, the processes I have identified may be said to have resulted in a remarkable variety of religious wars. For example, the Peasants' War pitted a broad coalition of princely and noble armies supported by the forces of the Swabian League against massive but ill-trained and poorly equipped peasant armies; the professionals won in a walkover, and subsequently exacted a harsh retribution. The French Civil Wars, by contrast, combined intracommunal bloodletting by informal crowds and locally mobilized militias with mercenary armies more or less equally matched on both sides of the conflict. By comparison with both of these, the Kappel Wars in Switzerland and the Schmalkaldic Wars in Germany seem like limited engagements between relatively small armies, involving little zealous popular engagement and even less destruction. The Eighty Years' War, the Thirty Years' War and the British Civil Wars represent still more variations. The point is that while these processes recurred in the run-up to the religious wars, they combined variously in different situations to produce divergent histories of war. We can expect to find a similar combination of recurrences and divergences, I think, when we try to understand the cultural politics of peace in Post-Reformation Europe.

In order to describe and account for the deeply contentious and politically messy peace that early modern Europeans eventually got, I would like to focus successively on three different sets of interactions at work in three very different arenas. First, I will consider the interactions of movement leaders, generals, and diplomats who ended the coordinated destruction of the religious wars, thereby making peace possible. Next, I will explore the patterns of domestic political interaction, involving variously authoritarian rulers – both civil and religious – and their 'dissident' subjects, that in the long term helped to structure coexistence in ways that neither side intended. Finally, I will focus on the informal actions and interactions that subtly and incrementally served to subvert the climate of intolerance that characterized Post-Reformation Europe.

## Making peace possible

Wars end in curious and unpredictable ways, and the religious wars of the sixteenth and seventeenth centuries are no exception. What makes civil wars especially unpredictable is that efforts to halt the warfare so frequently fail, and sooner or later, the violence and war resume (cf. Licklider (ed.), 1993; Walter, 2002). Still wars do end, and of course, the end of organized hostilities is what makes enduring peace possible. Though, in the minds of those specialists in coercion who prosecute them, wars and other lethal contests are undoubtedly about winning and losing, it is striking how difficult it is to indicate clear winners and losers at the end of these wars. With the exception of the first and the last of the entries in Table 1, all of the most prominent wars of religion ended with some form of compromise that was expressed in the terms of a truce, an edict, or a treaty. And even in the exceptional cases, winning and losing was not as clear or as distinct as it might at first seem. In the case of the Peasants' War, to be sure, the defeat of the peasant armies was followed by a harsh repression and most of the rebels' religious innovations were quickly undone (esp. Blickle, 1981, 1992). But recent German historiography suggests that the defeated peasants nevertheless won important concessions, especially in the form of legal institutions and processes that, *mirabile dictu*, afforded peasants and their agents the prospect of at least some satisfaction of their grievances (e.g. Schulze, 1984; Trossbach, 1987; Luebke, 1997).

As Table 1 suggests, then, the bulk of the wars of religion ended with some kind of formal settlement, though many of the attempted settlements proved to be unstable. The first of these compromise settlements – the Kappel treaties in Switzerland and the Peace of Augsburg in Germany – established an authoritarian pattern that eventually came to be expressed as a legal principle: *cuius regio, eius religio* [roughly: whose rule, his religion] (for Switzerland: Gordon, 2002; for Germany: Hughes, 1992). In the Swiss case, this meant that for the sake of preserving peace within their Confederation, each of the constituent territories was empowered to choose to be either Reformed or Catholic, thus insuring that religious authority, like political sovereignty, was decisively fragmented within the Confederation. In the German case, following a much longer history of struggle and intermittent warfare, the emperor, Charles V, effectively gave up his claim to enforce religious uniformity in the Empire as a whole and for the sake of Peace empowered his brother and successor to accept the principle that the constituent units of the Empire – the princely territories and the imperial cities – could choose either Lutheranism or Catholicism. Thus the Holy Roman Empire, too, institutionalized a fragmented cultural sovereignty that mirrored the fragmentation and layering of political sovereignty in much of central Europe.

The next round of religious war, which was concentrated in France and the Low Countries, produced a series of similarly ambiguous and, in the French case especially, less durable outcomes (For France: Jouanna et al., 1998; Collins, 1995. For the Low Countries: Parker, 1985; Benedict et al., 1999). Each of a long and destructive series of nine civil wars in France ended with the formal negotiation and promulgation of an edict that recognized legally what many in Latin Christendom at the time considered unthinkable: the coexistence of not only of two different faiths or 'confessions', but of two separate institutional churches, the Roman and the Reformed. The eighth of these edicts, the Edict of Nantes (1598), is the most famous because it proved the most durable; it institutionalized complex mechanisms for peacefully resolving disputes between the two religious groups, and it included secret amendments providing for the fortification of some forty Reformed strongholds at government expense. After the assassination of Henry IV, the royal governments of both Louis XIII and Louis XIV systematically undermined the provisions of the Edict of Nantes long before Louis XIV finally revoked the Edict in 1685. But it is hard even then to declare the autocratic king an unequivocal winner because the war Louis XIV subsequently waged against the so-called Camisards in the south failed to eliminate the Protestants and ended in a stalemate more than twenty years later (Joutard (ed.), 1976/1994).

The outcome of the religious wars in the Low Countries was only slightly less ambiguous. There, too, the first round of conflict ended briefly with an attempt to accommodate multiple faiths within a composite princely domain, but the general Pacification of Ghent (1576) clearly failed to bring about reconciliation when the opposing sides signed separate agreements in order to mobilize for war. At the beginning of the seventeenth century, the combatants negotiated a much longer Twelve-Year Truce (1609-1621), but since the war once again resumed, the whole of the intermittent struggle has traditionally been framed as the Eighty Years' War. In this case, the wars ended with two partial victories, which is also to say, two partial defeats. By the Treaty of Münster, the Spanish king finally recognized the independence of the rebellious territories, which in turn gave up their efforts to re-conquer the south; both sides thereby gave up on their long-standing goal of reuniting the seventeen Low Countries territories.

The enormously complicated and massively destructive Thirty Years' War was also ended by a negotiated settlement: The Peace of Westphalia, which was actually a composite of two treaties signed simultaneously in Osnabrück and Münster, took years to negotiate and involved more than 150 emissaries from polities great and small throughout Europe (On the war see Wilson, 2009; on the treaty Croxton & Tischer, 2002). Though much more elaborate, its provisions in many ways simply replicated or made minor adjustments to the earlier Peace of Augsburg, especially with regard to the question of religious sovereignty and the principle of *cuius regio, eius religio*. But the broad array of its signatories as well as its durability have led generations of scholars to regard the Peace of Westphalia as an important turning point in European history as well as a signal of the end of the age of religious wars. Indeed, for the next 150 years, it locked into place the layered sovereignties of the German Empire, and it modeled for generations of rulers to come a new system of international relations.

Finally, in the English Civil War, the Puritans' New Model Army under the command of Cromwell actually won a decisive victory over the forces of Charles I in 1648 (for a general survey Bennett, 1997; also: Woolrych, 2002). Then, having executed the king, abolished the monarchy and disestablished the Anglican Church in 1649, they went on to crush both the Irish Confederates (1650) and the Scottish Covenanters (1651) in order to consolidate their power in all three of the kingdoms that constituted British monarchy. But military success was followed within the next decade by political failure and gave way not only to a restoration of the monarchy in all three kingdoms, but the re-establishment of the Anglican Church. Indeed, unambiguous winners and losers are hard to find in Europe's religious wars.

## Structuring coexistence

Just as the formal outcomes of religious wars generally defied the intentions of the combatants, so also the structures of political and religious authority that emerged from the age of religious wars rarely conformed to anyone's vision of peace: Neither the authoritarian vision of divinely ordained political order and religious purity nor the alternative, idealized vision of concord and reconciliation. On the contrary, the structures of peaceful coexistence that eventually emerged in Post-Reformation Europe were more clearly the *unintended consequence* of an on-going and deeply contentious political process. Here the principal actors were not the military and political elites who prosecuted the wars or the diplomats who negotiated the peace settlements, but rather a variety of regional and local rulers and their religiously dissident subjects.

Though, as I have suggested, unambiguous victors are hard to find we should nevertheless start with the conditions that are created when political and religious authorities nevertheless claimed at least partial victory, or, as in the much of Mediterranean Europe, they never faced a serious armed challenge. To the extent that such political victories, however transient or partial they may have been, were paired with aggressively authoritarian claims to exclusive religious truth and communal purity, we can describe this outcome as active *repression*. Not surprisingly, active repression entailed enormous costs for dissident subjects, including not only destruction of lives and property, but also large flows of forced migration. Massive dislocations occurred, for example, in the Spanish Habsburg domains in both Iberia and the southern Low Countries, in the Austrian Habsburg domain in Bohemia, in France following the revocation of the Edict of Nantes, and even as late as 1723 in the Archbishopric of Salzburg (for Salzburg: Walker, 1992). Lest we conclude from this list of examples that such systematic intolerance and repression was the exclusive domain of Roman Catholic rulers, we should note similarly aggressive repression was aimed at Anabaptist and Catholic minorities in the city-states of Bern and Zürich and, of course, at the Catholic majority in Ireland. Recent research demonstrates, however, the profound limits of even determined and sustained repression. This is evident, for example, in the refusal of ordinary Spanish subjects (both in Iberia and in the New World) to participate in the repressive process organized by the Inquisition, and the inability of ecclesiastical courts to track down and eliminate determined dissidents in either the Catholic Low Countries or Protestant Bern (Melammed, 1999; Perry, 1996; Schwartz, 2008; Furner, 1998). In this sense, we can say that even the most repressive claims to religious uniformity typically mask the reality of very informal patterns of underground or secretive coexistence.

The far more common outcome of war and on-going religious struggle in the early modern period was a more equivocal victory and, by extension, a more circumscribed claim to religious uniformity. In such cases, we can describe the outcome in terms of *confessional privilege*, which entails the establishment of a privileged church enjoying an official monopoly on public religious practice. Though officially intolerant of the public expression of religious differences, such an arrangement excluded active persecution of dissident groups as long as they remained officially invisible and did not disturb public order; in addition, both the Union of Utrecht in the Northern Netherlands and the Treaty of Osnabrück in Germany specifically articulated an individual right to freedom of religious conscience, which effectively proscribed any form of heresy prosecution. To be sure, for those who nevertheless visibly asserted their 'dissident' religious identities, such an arrangement usually entailed the cost of official exclusion from political office, special fees or taxes, or even bribes to corrupt officials. To those who had previously been threatened with persecution or exile, however, the costs of official inequality and confessional privilege seemed like a reasonable price to pay for peace in places as diverse as the British monarchies, the Dutch Republic, and the constituent parts of the German Empire (Spufford (ed.), 1995; Spaans, 2002; Kaplan, 2007; Whaley, 1985).

An equally prominent outcome in post-Reformation Europe was a *parity system* in which the state pledged to guarantee the security of each officially recognized group and, by extension, granted a privileged arena of cultural self-regulation to more than one religious group. A parity regime, within which each group, regardless of size, was empowered to institutionalize its ideological principles internally while also participating in public affairs, was obviously an attractive prospect – indeed, it might even be considered the Holy Grail – for previously endangered or persecuted minorities. Such a parity regime, established in France by the Edict of Nantes in 1598, had obviously been fatally weakened by the time Louis XIV officially revoked the Edict in 1685, but multi-confessional parity nevertheless proved quite durable in various other settings: in German imperial cities, like Augsburg, and Swiss territories, like Thurgau, and for a time at least, in the massive domain of the composite Kingdom of Poland and Lithuania (Garrisson, 1998; Grandjean & Roussel (eds.), 1998; François, 1991; Head, 2001; Tazbir, 1973). But perhaps most importantly, both the Second Kappel Treaty in Switzerland and the Peace of Westphalia in Germany applied the parity principal to political relations at the level of the confederacy and the empire, respectively. As a consequence, in these notoriously complicated composite states a parity system regulated the political relations among religiously divided rulers, while confessional privilege and even sometimes active repression characterized the relations of local or territorial rulers and their dissident subjects.

In addition to these general systems of religious coexistence, Europe's ruler also frequently negotiated *ad-hoc* arrangements with specific groups of religiously 'different' subjects. Perhaps the most famous of these are the ghettos within which a variety of Italian rulers, including the Papacy, both recognized the difference and legitimated the self-regulation of their Jewish subjects (Israel, 1985; Head, 1990; cf. Johnson, 1998). Louis XIV struck a similar deal with the Jewish community in the city of Metz, while in the wake of the Thirty Years' War he guaranteed the security and legitimated the religious identities and corporate worship of his newly acquired Lutheran subjects in Alsace – this, *nota bene*, at the same time as he was ratcheting up his harassment of the Reformed population elsewhere in his composite state (Collins, 1995, pp. 100-105). Such special arrangements, which we can usefully call examples of *ad-hoc tolerance*, were the result of mutual agreement and can be found in virtually every polity in Post-Reformation Europe, especially in the form of embassy chapels which became privileged spaces for 'private' worship (Kaplan, 2002a).

On a much broader scale, the Ottoman Empire combined an established Islam with formal recognition and corporative self-regulation for specific groups of Jews and Christians throughout Southeastern Europe. Despite the inflammatory and religiously polarizing rhetoric that characterized the intermittent warfare between the Ottoman Empire and various coalitions in Christian Europe, this so-called *millet* system preserved a remarkably peaceful and durable pattern of religious coexistence in the Balkans through the end of the eighteenth century (see Braude & Lewis (eds.), 1982; Adanir, 2001; Barkey, 2008). Such *ad-hoc tolerance* should not be considered a free pass, however; in most cases, it entailed both political disabilities and financial costs, and it invariably required recognition of the superiority of the dominant religious group. Not least of all, it entailed the insecurity of knowing that the 'sovereign' who granted such favors could also, in principle, revoke them at will. Still, by the end of the old regime ad-hoc tolerance had become the preferred mechanism for softening the roughest edges and resolving most glaring incongruities of official intolerance. Thus, it was that even the kings of France and Austria issued edicts of tolerance for formerly persecuted minorities in the 1780s.

Mapping out and documenting this range of variation in European historical experience is itself an on-going process. Nevertheless, Figure 1 represents a conceptual map of what I think we have learned about the range of variation evident in European experience. Rather than constructing a single continuum that ranges from repression to 'liberty', I want to argue that the patterns of religious coexistence during and after the age of religious wars varied along at least two dimensions, both of which must be seen as the product of the contentious political interactions between authoritarian rulers, religious and/or civil, and their religiously diverse subjects. On one hand, the *cultural politics* of

Europe's many political regimes varied significantly in the extent to which they were inclusive or exclusive of religiously different groups among their subjects – that is, whether they institutionalized a strong alignment with a particular set of cultural authorities or not. On the other hand, the *salience of religious identities* within the realm of public politics varied significantly; here I think of the extent to which religious differences were publicly visible and they not only demarcated the boundaries of official inclusion and exclusion in the political process, but served also to regulate routine access to occupations and social services like poor relief or education. Such variations should not be conflated with the cultural politics of regimes or the alignments of rulers with particular cultural authorities; they reflect instead the degree to which alternative alignments between 'dissident' cultural authorities and ordinary people made a credible or enforceable claim to collective recognition in public life or not.

Figure 1: patterns of religious coexistence in Europe

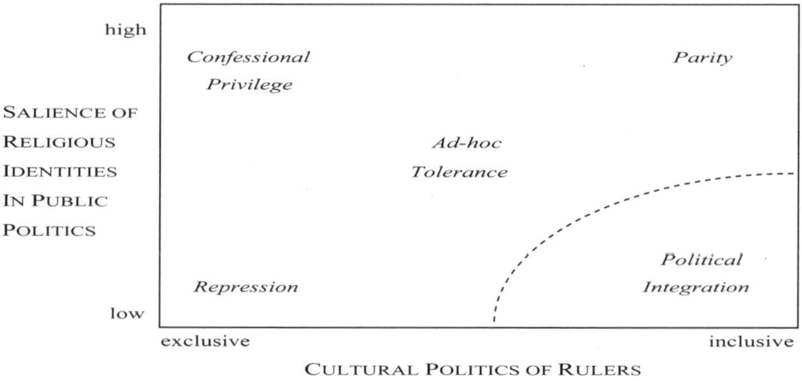


To my mind, this kind of conceptual map is primarily useful as a tool for locating and tracking the *historical experiences of specific religious groups or polities* within a larger comparative context in order to ask sharper questions about how we can describe and account for those experiences. Figures 2 and 3 illustrate, for example, the stunning changes over time in the structures of religious coexistence in the Northern Netherlands and France, initially during the initial wars of religion and later during the ensuing period of relative peace. Having started out with a common experience of brutal repression in the 1550s, the Dutch Republic and France moved during the war years toward confessional privilege and parity, respectively. In the course of the seventeenth century, however, as French policy moved decisively back toward active repression of Reformed Protestants, the Dutch Republic moved toward ad-hoc tolerance, gradually integrating Lutherans, Mennonites and Remonstrants (Arminians) into public life while formally excluding Catholics and Jews from political participation (Spaans, 2002). By contrast, the Ottoman Empire maintained a remarkably stable pattern of ad-hoc tolerance throughout the early modern period.

Figure 2: Religious coexistence in the Northern Netherlands and France, Phase I

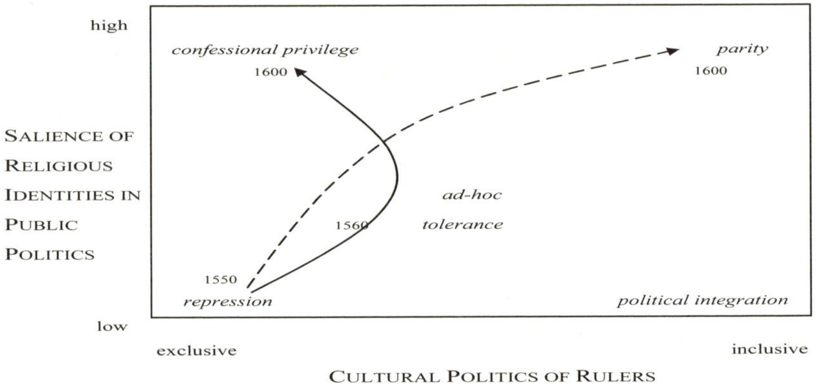


Figure 3: Religious coexistence in the Northern Netherlands and France, Phase II

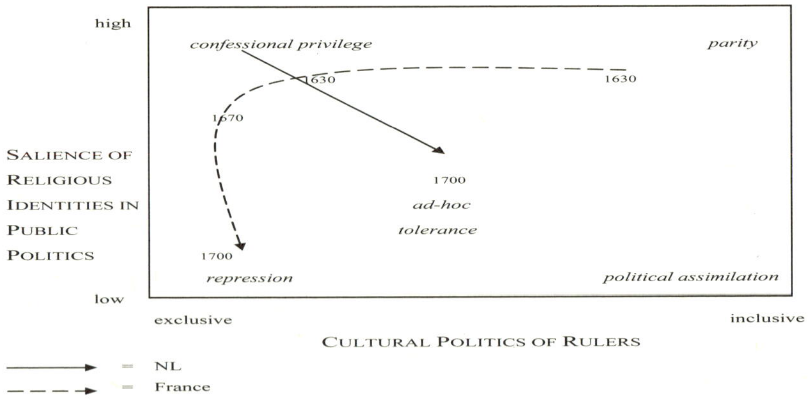

For our purposes here, however, the conceptual map also highlights the theoretical possibility of another type of religious coexistence that many of us might today consider ideal, but was nowhere evident in early modern Europe – something I term *political integration* but we might also describe it as the separation of church and state. Theoretically, even publicly evident differences in religious belief and practice do not, under a regime of political integration, serve as markers of inclusion or exclusion in public politics – that is, religious identities lose their political salience – while the privilege of corporative self-regulation is granted equally to all religiously different groups within the polity. Without being able to elaborate this point fully, let me at least suggest that the striking absence of this outcome from our catalogue of early modern historical experiences is due, I think, to two very different, yet complementary factors. On one hand, the rulers of Europe's composite states routinely used the inequalities entailed by selective privileges as an effective instrument of indirect rule as well as a powerful lever in political bargaining. On the other hand, a broad range of religiously different subjects and their variously constituted leaders actively resisted an official divorce between religious and political identities because of the obvious cost in terms of corporate identity and political clout that such a divorce entails.

## Subverting intolerance

As we have already seen, the most obvious outcome of the wars of religion was a general institutionalization of official intolerance, for even where a parity system or ad-hoc tolerance recognized multiple faiths, they still excluded other 'dissenters'. In order to move beyond the *official story* of selective privilege, discrimination, and intolerance, however, we have to move beyond the public realm of contentious politics to the more private or at least less visible realm of subversive action. Indeed, it is in the largely hidden historical process of subverting official intolerance that a whole host of European actors laid the foundations of religious peace and pluralism in modern Europe. Excavating this hidden history is not easy, of course, but its significance is especially evident under the conditions of active repression – where religious difference has been criminalized and where simple survival is at stake. Under conditions of severe repression, in fact, simple survival may be considered the ultimate revenge (See Te Brake, 2009).

Looking at evidence from settings as diverse as Spain, the city-state of Bern, the southern Netherlands (first under Spanish, later Austrian control), Ireland and France after the Revocation of the Edict of Nantes, we can discern a variety of common survival strategies among officially illegal religious groups (in addition to works cited earlier: Schwartz, 2001; Goosens, 1997-1998; Power & Whelan (eds.), 1990; Hanlon, 1993). The first and most obvious is *secrecy*, making sure that acts of religious devotion remain private and collective worship remains invisible or at least beyond the reach of the law. In some parts of Europe, 'dissident' worship within *schuilkerken* (or hidden churches) was disguised only by a formal facade, but in other places, strict secrecy could be urgently necessary (Kaplan, 2002b). Beyond collective secrecy, however, there is the more individual practice of *dissimulation* – that is, hiding individual dissent under the cover of apparent conformity. This is, of course, the specter that consistently haunted inquisitorial courts as they insistently examined the beliefs of Moriscos, Conversos and other suspected 'heretics' (Melammed, 1999; Spaans, 2002). But dissimulation was a practical necessity for officially proscribed 'dissenters' who nevertheless aspired to participate in the public affairs of less repressive regimes.

In the long run, the survival of secretive religious groups often required (or was at least aided by) a certain amount of *casuistry* – that is, making formal exemptions or adaptations to the ideologically driven rules of religious purity that would normally be required under conditions of greater liberty (See especially Furner's (1998) use of this term). This is actually the specter that often haunted the spiritual leaders of persecuted groups, like John Calvin who was often critical of French Huguenots who, prior to the Religious Wars, were willing to sacrifice religious purity or practice dissimulation for the sake of survival. But the ultimate weapon that a wide variety of dissenters deployed in the face of official intolerance was *private education.* Informal or private education was more often the work of women among strictly secretive groups than among officially recognized minorities where the European patriarchal norm was more like to prevail. But in either case, private education had the powerful effect of limiting or counteracting exposure to official indoctrination and blunting the force of active confessionalization.

But the survival of religious minorities (or even persecuted majorities as in Ireland) is rarely, if ever, a solo performance by the dissenting individuals or groups in question. It clearly depends to some extent on the behavior of others, not only rulers but third parties. First, and perhaps foremost, it is enabled by a certain degree of *indifference* to officially inscribed religious differences. Official intolerance, which is rooted in an alliance between religious authorities and political officials, entails obviously variable levels of effort to police the identity boundaries that have been activated in conflict and exacerbated by violence and war. But especially under conditions of active repression, authorities clearly restrict transactions across the disputed boundaries. Indifference to these officially inscribed differences might simply entail doing business as usual with 'others' in the marketplace, but under extreme conditions (like those imposed by the existence of inquisitorial courts) indifference may well entail an active and potentially dangerous refusal to condemn 'others' as required by law (see Schwartz, 2001, 2009). But group survival usually entails as well the active *connivance* of others outside the group in order to subvert official policies of discrimination and prosecution. Here one thinks not only of bribes paid to 'corrupt' officials responsible for the enforcement of intolerance, but also of a variety of inter-religious family strategies, such as intermarriage, designed to preserve the property of illegal dissenters, like Catholics in Ireland and Protestants in France (see Kooi, 2002; Whelan, 1990; Luria, 1996).

Finally, we should by no means underestimate the importance of *everyday practices of toleration* – by which I mean the active appreciation of religious differences. Something like 'genuine toleration' – as opposed to *ad-hoc tolerance* – is often seen primarily as a intellectual or cognitive attribute of properly 'enlightened' individual minds, but it is equally important a social and political practice. Here I think of the way religiously competitive groups routinely, if reluctantly, shared worship spaces, usually in small or poor communities which could not afford to construct separate buildings. There were also, in some places, traditions in which competing groups actually attend their rivals' worship services on special days in the liturgical year. Such relationships were not easy, especially at first or in the context of significant polarization; at times, they might even require mediation by third parties in disputes over church architecture and the arrangement of the worship space (e.g. Z'Graggen, 1999). But such everyday practices of toleration, which category may also include behaviors I described earlier as indifference or connivance, can become over time routine behaviors, the memory of which can even seem a bit nostalgic when competition intensifies or violence recurs (Doumanis, 2001). I do not, by any means, want to suggest that coexistence always lends itself to such mutual appreciation; the official historical record is replete with instances of resurgent conflict and effectively policed boundaries that indicate the contrary. I want simply to suggest that to date we have only just begun to excavate this largely hidden history of alternative cultural experiences, countervailing political processes and subversive social behaviors.

## Accommodating difference

So what can we learn by expanding the historical dimension of the problems posed in the introduction? By way of conclusion, I will highlight just a few possible answers to this question, beginning with a historical correction. Embedded in this headlong review of the history of war and peace in Reformation and post-Reformation Europe, there is what I believe to be an important, but contentious, historical generalization: in the face of a pervasive pattern of official intolerance in post-Reformation times, there emerged an equally pervasive pattern of peaceful coexistence among religiously 'different' groups within common political boundaries. In other words, despite official appearances, peaceful religious coexistence was more clearly the rule than the exception in early modern Europe. This generalization is important to us today in at least three complementary ways.

In the first instance, it exposes the limits of much of the traditional wisdom on modern European history. On one hand, the positivist traditions of strictly disciplinary historical scholarship have privileged and replicated the claims – or, in other words, the dominant discourses – of authoritarian rulers by following the relatively easy path of exhaustive research in official records and archives. On the other hand, cultural critiques of traditional historicism, in exposing the prejudices and silences of both religious and political claims to authority through textual criticism, have nevertheless overstated the hegemony of cultural and political authorities in European history. In order to move definitively beyond the authoritarian perspective of rulers, it seems to me, we need once again to dare to generalize, but this time, not in order to posit a putative *mainline* or *norm* of European experience, but rather to describe and account for the range of its diversity through deliberately cross-disciplinary and comparative studies of the sort sketched out in the introduction. Actually seeing and accounting for that diversity requires us, however, to focus on the often unintended consequences of the historical *interaction* of authoritative claims/discourses and challenging or dissenting counterclaims, not just one or the other.

Secondly, scholars of modern Europe are habitually, if not as a matter of principle, reluctant to reach beyond the almost impenetrable boundary that academic discourse has constructed between 'tradition' and 'modernity'. Yet the simultaneous emergence of both authoritarian intolerance and a countervailing, if messy, pluralism in pre-modern or traditional Europe demands that we transgress the tradition/modernity dichotomy as we face the increasing prospect of religious conflict and violence in this new millennium. However much we might imagine religious freedom to be one of the most fundamental and universal of 'modern' human rights, such rights remain deeply contested today, even in European democracies. What the history of religious peace and coexistence in early modern Europe teaches, however, is that under the conditions of both official and popular intolerance and even active repression – which more accurately reflects the circumstances of the majority of mankind today than our idealized visions of universally recognized rights – diversity and pluralism can not only survive but also prosper. In short, the political and cultural history of post-Reformation provide us with an invaluable opportunity to discover the recurrent processes that make for peaceful religious coexistence in the context of polarization, violence and even war.

Finally, with regard to the cases that are focused on in this volume on, it is clear that in the early modern period the Kingdom of France and the Dutch Republic experienced very divergent histories of religious coexistence, with important differences evident not only across these very diverse polities but within them and over time. It is equally clear, by extension, that although in the modern period they all moved toward the institutional separation of church and state, their journeys in that general direction began from very different starting points and the multiple actors whose interaction moved them in that common direction carried with them the very different political-cultural legacies of their respective old regimes. Indeed, from the perspective of an early-modern historian, the various modes of incorporation represent not only the cultural and discursive legacies of differently conflicted histories as represented in contentious and partial national narratives, but the specific legal, structural and political legacies of treaties, constitutions, and repertoires of contention. For example, the universalist French mode and the consociational Dutch mode of the modern era are deeply embedded in the practices and institutions of French absolutism and Dutch republicanism, as filtered through very different histories of political revolution and democratization. Indeed, perhaps the most enduring obstacle to understanding the on-going historical process of accommodating religious and cultural differences is the academic myth that national state formation and democratization wiped the 'traditional' slate clean and set the stage for unprecedented challenges, like multiculturalism, in a fundamentally 'modern' world.

## References


Adanir, F. (2001). *Religious communities and ethnic groups under imperial sway: Ottoman and Habsburg lands in comparison*. Paper presented at the Netherlands Institute for Advanced Study, Wassenaar.

Barkey, K. (2008). *Empire of difference: The Ottomans in comparative perspective*. Cambridge, NY: Cambridge University Press.

Benedict, Ph. et al. (eds.) (1999). *Reformation, revolt and civil war in France and the Netherlands 1555–1585*. Amsterdam: Koninklijke Nederlandse Akademie van Wetenschappen.

Bennett, M. (1997). *The civil wars in Britain and Ireland 1638–1651*. Oxford: Blackwell Publishers.

Blickle, P. (1981). *The revolution of 1525: The German peasants' war from a new perspective*. Baltimore: The Johns Hopkins University Press.

Blickle, P. (1992). *Communal reformation: The quest for salvation in sixteenth-century Germany*. Atlantic Highlands, NJ: Humanities Press.

Braude, B. & Lewis, B. (eds.). (1982). *Christians and Jews in the Ottoman empire: The functioning of a plural society*. New York: Holmes and Meier.

Cameron, E. (1991). *The European reformation*. Oxford: Clarendon Press.

Collins, J.B. (1995). *The state in early modern France: New approaches to European history*. Cambridge: Cambridge University Press.

Croxton, D. & Tischer, A. (2002). *The peace of Westphalia: A historical dictionary*. Westport, Conn.: Greenwood Press.

Doumanis, N. (2001). *Pretty histories of neighborliness: Idyllic memories of mixed communities among Greek Orthodox Ottomans and modern Bosnian Muslims*. Paper presented at the Netherlands Institute for Advanced Study, Wassenaar.

François, E. (1991). *Die unsichtbare Grenze: Protestanten und Katholiken in Augsburg 1648–1806*. Sigmaringen: Jan Thorbeke Verlag.

Furner, M. (1998). *The repression and survival of Anabaptism in the Emmental, Switzerland, 1659–1743*. PhD-thesis Cambridge University.

Garrisson, J. (1998). *L'Edit de Nantes: Chronique d'une paix attendue*. Paris: Fayard.

Goosens, A. (1997-1998). *Les Inquisitions modernes dans les Pays-Bas méridionaux (1520–1633)*. Bruxelles: Éditions de l'Université de Bruxelles.

Gordon, B. (2002). *The Swiss Reformation*. Manchester: Manchester University Press.

Grandjean, M. & Roussel, B. (eds.). (1998). *Coexister dans l'intolérance: L'édit de Nantes (1598)*. Geneva: Labor et Fides.

Hanlon, G. (1993). *Confession and community in seventeenth-century France: Catholic and Protestant coexistence in Aquitaine*. Philadelphia: University of Pennsylvania Press.

Head, R.C. (1990). Religious boundaries and the inquisition in Venice: Trials of Jews and Judaizers, 1548–1580. *Journal of Medieval and Renaissance Studies, 20*(2), 175–204.

Head, R.C. (2001). *Negotiating co-existence through institutions and practice in early modern Europe: The Thurgau, 1520–1712*. Paper presented at the Netherlands Institute for Advanced Study, Wassenaar.

Hughes, M. (1992). *Early modern Germany 1477–1806*. Philadelphia: University of Pennsylvania Press.

Israel, J.I. (1985). *European Jewry in the age of mercantilism 1550–1750*. Oxford: Oxford University Press.

Johnson, E. (1998). *'Sons of the serving maid': Conflict and cohesion in the ghettoes of the contat Venaissin 1555–1791*. Paper presented to the Social Science History Association, Chicago (Il).

Jouanna, A. et al. (1998). *Histoire et dictionnaire des guerres de religion*. Paris: Robert Laffont.

Joutard, Ph. (ed.). (1994) *Les Camisards*. Paris: Editions Gallimard. (original work published 1976).

Kaplan, B.J. (2002a). Diplomacy and domestic devotion: Embassy

chapels and the toleration of dissent in early modern Europe. *Journal of Early Modern History, 6*(4), 341–61.
Kaplan, B.J. (2002b). Fictions of privacy: House chapels and the spatial accommodation of religious dissent in early modern Europe. *American Historical Review, 107*(4), 1031–64.
Kaplan, B.J. (2007). *Divided by faith: Religious conflict and the practice of toleration in early modern Europe*. Cambridge, MA: Harvard University Press.
Kooi, C. (2002). Paying off the sheriff: Strategies of Catholic toleration in Golden Age Holland. In R. Po-Chia Hsia & H.F.K. van Nierop (eds.), *Calvinism and religious toleration in the Dutch Golden Age* (pp. 87–101). Cambridge: Cambridge University Press.
Licklider, R. (ed.). (1993). *Stopping the killing: How civil wars end.* New York: New York University Press.
Luebke, D.M. (1997). *His majesty's rebels: Communities, factions, and rural revolt in the Black Forest 1725–1745*. Ithaca: Cornell University Press.
Luria, K.P. (1996). The politics of Protestant conversion to Catholicism in seventeenth-century France. In P. van der Veer (ed.), *Conversion to modernities: The globalization of Christianity* (pp. 23–46). New York: Routledge.
Melammed, R.L. (1999). *Heretics or daughters of Israel? The crypto-Jewish women of Castile*. New York: Oxford University Press.
Parker, G. (1985). *The Dutch revolt.* Harmondsworth: Penguin.
Perry, M.E. (1996). Behind the veil: Moriscas and the politics of resistance and survival. In M.S. Sánchez & A. Saint-Saëns (eds.), *Spanish women in the golden age: Images and realities* (pp. 37–53). Westport, Conn.: Greenwood Press.
Power, T.P. & Whelan, K. (eds.). (1990) *Endurance and emergence: Catholics in Ireland in the eighteenth century*. Dublin: Irish Academic Press.
Schulze, W. (1984). Peasant resistance in sixteenth- and seventeenth-century Germany in a European context. In K. von Greyerz (ed.), *Religion, politics and social protest* (pp. 61–98). London: George Allen and Unwin.
Schwartz, S.B. (2001) *Roots of popular toleration in the Hispanic world.* Paper presented at the Netherlands Institute for Advanced Study, Wassenaar.
Schwartz, S.B. (2008). *All can be saved: Religious tolerance and salvation in the Iberian Atlantic world.* New Haven: Yale University

Press.
Spaans, J. (2002) Violent dreams, peaceful coexistence: On the absence of religious violence in the Dutch Republic. *De Zeventiende Eeuw, 18*(2), 149–66.
Spufford, M. (ed.). (1995). *The world of rural dissenters 1520–1725*. Cambridge: Cambridge University Press.
Tazbir, J. (1979). *A state without stakes: Polish religious toleration in the sixteenth and seventeenth centuries*. New York: Kosciuszko Foundation.
Te Brake, W. (1998). *Shaping history: Ordinary people in European politics 1500–1700*. Berkeley-Los Angeles: University of California Press.
Te Brake, W. (2009). Emblems of coexistence in a confessional world. In S. Dixon, D. Freist & M. Greengrass (eds.), *Living with religious diversity in Early Modern Europe* (53-79). Aldershot: Ashgate.
Tracy, J.D. (1999). *Europe's reformations 1450–1650*. Lanham, MD: Rowman and Littlefield.
Trossbach, W. (1987). *Soziale Bewegung und politische Erfahrung: Bäuerlicher Protest in hessischen Territorien 1648–1806*. Weingarten: Drumlin Verlag.
Walker, M. (1992). *The Salzburg transaction: Expulsion and redemption in eighteenth-century Germany*. Ithaca, NY: Cornell University Press.
Walter, B.F. (2002). *Committing to peace: The successful settlement of civil wars*. Princeton: Princeton University Press.
Whaley, J. (1985). *Religious toleration and social change in Hamburg 1529–1819*. Cambridge: Cambridge University Press.
Whelan, K. (1990). The Catholic community in eighteenth-century county Wexford. In T.P. Power & K. Whelan (eds.), *Endurance and emergence: Catholics in Ireland in the Eighteenth Century* (pp. 129–170). Dublin: Irish Academic Press.
Wilson, P.H. (2009). *The Thirty Years War*. Cambridge: Harvard University Press.
Woolrych, A. (2002). *Britain in revolution, 1625–1660*. Oxford: Oxford University Press.
Z'Graggen, B. (1999). *Tyrannenmord im Toggenburg: Fürstäbtyische Herrschaft und protestantischer Widerstand um 1600*. Zürich: Chronos Verlag.

## French *laïcité*, between national conflict and local compromises

### For an interactionist approach to the concept of political culture

Bérengère Massignon

The framework of analysis presented in the introduction helps stimulate a comparative approach on the integration of ethnic-religious diversity in European countries, particularly France and the Netherlands. Instead of 'essentializing' the culture of newcomers – in this case Muslims – as a factor explaining their difficulties of integration, it shifts the focus to the political culture of the host country, which is more or less exclusive with regard to differences. It is not difference, as such, that is an obstacle to integration but the manner in which it is constructed and interpreted according to the cultural codes and the greater or lesser tolerance of the host country to accept diversity. The political concept of nationality and citizenship works, as Brubaker (1992) has already indicated, as a factor of inclusion and exclusion. The issue of the role of women crystallizes cultural oppositions.

The question here is whether political culture amounts to maintaining a culturalist type analysis, essentializing in turn the culture of the host country and, in view of its intrinsic characteristics (homogeneity, stability and its global nature), conferring on it a monocausal explanatory character. Furthermore, the theoretical framework in the introduction borrows a developmentalist definition of political culture from Almond and Verba ([1963] 1989): the older the democracy, the more stable it is, and therefore the more susceptible a country is to be open towards diversity. Therefore, it is difficult to see how the political culture of a country can change, since the cultural variable is presented as an independent variable.

However, by leaving the field of a macro sociological analysis in order to present a micro sociological approach as inspired by the field of research on the management of religious diversity in French state schools with regard to the culture of *laïcité* among teachers, it seems possible to maintain the hypothesis of political culture while making it more complex. Staying within the framework of interactionist sociology, the object of this analysis is neither the culture of the newcomers nor that of the host country, but rather their interaction. I focused on the answers given by the French teaching body in response to students' demands concerning the expression of their religious affiliation (the wearing of religious symbols, taking days off for religious reasons, and the restriction of certain foods from the school canteen, for a description of the whole research project see Massignon, 2000). I wish to demonstrate, with the help of this example, that it is possible to illuminate the comprehensive rather than explanatory virtues of the term of political culture. Thus I depart from the developmentalist and systemo-functionalist assumptions that have guided the definition of political culture by Almond and Verba and the American School of political sociology, in favor of an interactionist approach to culture inspired by Clifford Geertz (1973). Culture is a structure for comprehension, a code, a system of meaning allowing a minimal congruence between actors; it is not a homogeneous whole implying similar conducts. Therefore, *laïcité*, which is a key concept in French political culture, can be reinstated 1. in its oppositions, conflicts and evolutions, and 2. by exploring the link between disciplinary practices and teachers' systems of beliefs.

### *Laïcité* in the French political culture: conflicts and evolutions

In France, *laïcité* constitutes a key concept of political culture, which can generally be qualified as universalist and monist (Wieviorka, 1996). It is founded, in other respects, on a very particular concept of politics. In fact, *laïcité*, under the Third Republic, was defined within a framework associating the autonomy of politics and its corollary, the privatization of religion. This combination was legitimized by a political philosophy affirming the superiority of the state as guardian of universal values and public interest against civil society threatened by particularisms (see the analyses of Nicolet, 1982 and Baudouin & Portier, 2001). This vision is particularly embodied by the 'Educational State'. State schools are the nodal point of socialization to the Republican ideal and national feeling. The student had to subjugate his or her allegiances to primary groups (family, religion, ethnicity, region) in order to progress, through instruction, to the universal, whose emblematic figure was the rational citizen who gave primary allegiance to the nation-state.

A French peculiarity, this obligation was not limited to newcomers from different religious, ethnic and national backgrounds, but extended to the entire French population, including the old Catholic majority. In fact, *laïcité* asserted itself in a conflictual manner that did not oppose natives and newcomers, but rather was a rift between those holding two concepts of the Nation, each of which laid claim to representing the whole country: the partisans of France as a Christian nation (*la France fille aînée de l'Église*), and those who promoted a France which was the beneficiary of the principles of 1789 (*La France patrie des droits de l'homme*). This internal rift within French political life was able to integrate the Jewish and Protestant religious minorities that supported *laïcité*, with the promise of an accepted pluralism and a secular definition of the Nation. Later, the Dreyfus Affair, the Great War, then the split between collaborators and *Resistants,* during the World War II, helped to integrate various European migrants who came to France at the end of the 19th century, and between the two world wars. Finally, class conflicts allowed the integration of migrant workers, namely the *Magrhébins*, during the 1960s and 1970s. Even if this process was hostile to the public expression of religious, linguistic, ethnic and regional differences, French political culture and *laïcité* acted as vectors of integration and of diversity (as long as this diversity remained private) and as a means of access to citizenship for minorities. France has a long history of internal and external conflicts which prompted the integration of newcomers. This fact questions the idea of political culture as a principle of homogeneity and stability. A dialogical conception of culture allows for the understanding of this specificity.

Nowadays, the Republican model is in crisis as it is challenged by deep transformations which affect all modern democracies. Those changes affect the French Republican model more profoundly (Baudouin & Portier, 2001): globalization favors other national models that are more compatible with the "consecration of civil society" (Gauchet, 1998), hedonist individualism, the "multiculturalization" of society, the expansion of moral relativism and post-modern values, and decentralized governance in an interdependent world. As Jean-Paul Willaime underlines, there was a 'laïcisation of *laïcité*' by an internal critique of the ideals of progress, science and reason that were the basis of a secular universalist utopia, as foundation of a transfer of sacredness in politics (Willaime, 1990, p. 195). In fact, all those evolutions affect a nation-state's authority. The state is the backbone of French national unity, self-consciousness and ability to act and move. It is often said that in France the state made the nation whereas in Germany, Italy or Poland the nation made the state. It is therefore no surprise that the debate in France over Muslim integration occurs in public schools, which was the backbone of French socialization to democracy during the Third Republic.

*Laïcité* has always been an object of social debate. It does not function as a uniform concept. There never was a homogeneous secular culture; *laïcité* is a melting pot concept at the cross roads of various intellectual contributions: spiritualism, positivism, socialism... (Nicolet, 1982; Ognier, 2001; see also Baubérot, 1990, 1999, 2004). There are different ways of understanding *laïcité* and applying it to the educational sphere. *Laïcité* was the object of a virulent conflict of interpretation producing a scrambling effect (Baubérot, 1996) in the century-old conflict between clericals and anti-clericals, pitting Catholics against secularists, the right against the left, in what Emile Poulat called the 'war between the two France' (Poulat, 1987). During the second half of the 20$^{th}$ century, the residue of this quarrel was the conflict over state financing for private religious schools. During the headscarves affair, it was the secularists and the political left –far more than the right wing parties- that were divided. They were caught between the necessity to exclude veiled schoolgirls in order to maintain the principle of *laïcité* in school and negotiating the secular rule in order to protect the freedom of conscience of the students and their chance for progressive integration into French society through state schooling. The ideological debate is far from settled (Molokotos-Liederman, 2000). At first a legal line came forth from the different opinions of the Council of State (*Conseil d'État*) and ministerial circulars. According to Maurice Barbier, these texts indicate a profound change affecting French *laïcité*. France has gone from a "*laïcité* as separation", founded on the division between the public/private spheres, the primacy of politics and the confinement of religion to the private sphere, to "*laïcité* as neutrality", founded on the acknowledgement of the pre-eminence of individual rights (Barbier, 1995, pp. 84-90). The law on religious signs of the 15$^{th}$ of March 2004 inverted the balance, which is proof of an instability between the two visions of *laïcité*.

French political culture has therefore, in its own particular way, recorded the mutations affecting all western democracies with the decline of the reason of state and the triumph of the belief in human rights. In a period of globalization, europeanization and the transformation of the role of nation-states, it is impossible to maintain an impenetrable political culture. Furthermore, political culture cannot be conceived as a permanent fact. It is evolving. In order to demonstrate its micro sociological mechanisms, one must leave the macro sociological analysis at a national level and examine the interaction between teachers and immigrant students in educational institutions, and more particularly the face to face relationship between teachers and students inside the classroom, between those who teach and those who are taught.

## The *laïcité* of teachers: from value to action

Here we examine the situation before the law of 2004 banning religious signs from public school to show the scope for accommodations and innovations of French secular political culture. *Laïcité* is not the only principle of action that guides the behavior of teachers faced with student demands to be allowed express their religion. Some requirements are difficult to conciliate. There is the necessity to maintain peace (hold the classroom and maintain order in the institution) and uphold their secular principles, while at the same time observing the principle of equality (equality of opportunity in the education system, equality of the sexes) and the necessity to integrate newcomers through state schools. Sometimes, this results in a '*laïcité* of indifference' and religion is put aside in order to achieve equality among students regardless of their religious origin. Managing religion is then achieved through a trivialization of the religious character of student demands. For example, the demand by Jewish and Muslim students for special meals to substitute for pork in school canteens are accepted since they can be likened to medical necessities and the fact that the students have to eat. The general introduction of self-service canteen offers a practical solution to these demands. In the negotiations over the wearing of the veil, before the law of 2004 banning them from public schools, teachers ended up proposing a compromise: the wearing of a headdress that has fewer religious connotations, such as a bonnet, a turban or a small colored headscarf. Therefore, this can be viewed as a characteristic the integration model *á la française*: the right to indifference rather than the right to difference.

Religious demands are managed at the disciplinary level: the Council of State condemned incidents of the wearing of veils because they disturbed public order and because there was a refusal to engage in dialogue with the teaching body. The law of March 2004 has hardened relations. The wearing of religious signs is totally excluded from state public schools, but the circular on its application maintains the principle of dialogue between teachers, the student and her family before any exclusion from school. What is at issue is the visibility of religious practices in the educational field. A headscarf is more visible than a small cross worn as jewelry. An empty school on the day which the Muslim feast *Eid* falls on is more visible than some Jewish students missing classes on Saturdays, in observance of the *Shabbat*, though both cases contravene the students' obligation to attend school. The numerical impact is therefore taken into account and it is unfair towards Islam in most cases, as Islamic students form the majority of the student body in educational institutions in certain suburban areas. Therefore, the number of students who observe Ramadan or wear veils introduces a relationship of force with the education authorities. However, the demands of Jewish students or those of practicing Catholics (a minority) fare better through their individual negotiations, which are facilitated by the existence of semi-official religious mediators such as the Catholic chaplain in secondary institutions or the local rabbi. Furthermore the parents of Jewish or Catholic students have a better command of the codes of educational institutions. This allows them to make their case through demands by petition or during the time of student registration at the beginning of the school year without disturbing the school order. Thus they avoid the protests and other violations of school discipline which Muslim students and their families sometimes engage in (for example, the refusal to make an official demand for the authorization of absences during Muslim religious holidays, which are provided for by the Official Bulletin of the Ministry of National Education). The codes of a democratic society weigh on the perception of religious expressions. What is troubling about veiled students is not the veil itself but rather the accompanying behavior inspired by religious fundamentalism such as the refusal for girls and boys to mix (in sports, in sex education during the natural sciences class), the refusal to accept the instruction of secular knowledge in sciences, philosophy, literature (e.g., refusing instruction on the Theory of Evolution theories, or refusal to study 'blasphemous' authors like Voltaire). Thus feminist principles condemn the veil as a sign of female submission whereas the *kippa* and the Sikh turban do not have the same sexist connotation. Feminism and *laïcité* can sometimes be used as an argument to support implicitly a mundane and acceptable form of racism, which some authors have denounced (Guénifi-Souilamas & Macé, 2006).

*Laïcité* in school appears here as a space of interactions and competition for the definition of what is the legitimate practice in school as a disciplinary space. The explanation through culture does not exclude an analysis of the structures of domination of teachers versus students and of French natives versus immigrants.

Before the law of March 2004, teachers managed the religious demands of students on a case-by-case basis, even if in the name of *laïcité* they would like to refuse all of them. This has led to an implicit hierarchy of religions, which does not correspond with the egalitarian secular beliefs of teachers. It is the result of the necessity to maintain order in school while safeguarding and teaching the values of the host society. This hierarchy combines the criteria of tradition (favorable to the majority religion and to the old and established Protestant and Jewish religions recognized by the Napoleonic *Concordat*), of integration (applied negatively mostly to Muslim students, since Buddhists are not seeking visibility of their practice in public spaces), of notoriety (applied to 'minor minorities' religions like Sikhs or Seventh-Day Adventists) and of dangerousness (applied to sects). The criterion of notoriety can sometimes work to the benefit of minor religious groups: their religious expression is considered as mostly exotic more than religious and therefore is ignored; it was the case for the Sikhs turban which was tolerated before the Law on religious signs of 2004. During the preparation of this Law by different governmental and parliamentary commission, the case of Sikhs was forgotten. They were not consulted. But they have strongly mobilized on national and above all international plan since the voting of the Law which changed the overall perception of the turban from an ethnic sign to a religious one. The criterion for integration is ambiguous because it shows the complexity in the perception of difference as well as its stereotypes. As Michèle Tribalat (1995) pointed out, immigrants from the Maghreb are rather well integrated, because they speak French in the private sphere, have mixed marriages and take part in elections, at least more than Portuguese migrants for instance. However, they are seen as less integrated into French society than Asians, even though the latter come from afar and have stronger communal ties, something that is generally conceived negatively in the French context.

The secular culture of teachers can be analyzed as an element of their perception of reality (even teachers who are hostile to excluding students are against their being allowed to wear veils, this being either a sign of Muslim fundamentalism, or, more frequently, a sign of the oppression of women). However, an explanation just referring to the strongly affirmed secular culture of teachers (Aubert, 1984; Aubert, Ozouf & Ozouf 1987; Bianconi, 1987) is not sufficient to clarify the diversity of disciplinary practices with regard to the religious demands of students from one school to another and, sometimes even, from one class to another in the same institution. It is necessary to construct a theoretical space between long-term culture and the short-term situation by defining gradual levels of analysis: cultural systems (and their relationship to socialization), attitude systems, conduct systems and situations of interaction. The notion of culture, therefore, finds its heuristic importance as a link between the individual and the collective. It is conceived as a whole of internalized norms. The more we draw near a micro-sociological level of analysis, the more identities become individualized into conducts.

We can draw two behavioral ideal-types by going back to the Weberian classifications, leading to two visions of *laïcité* and of the relation between law and practice. There are teachers acting according to a value-based rational and developing an ethic of conviction: in the name of *laïcité*, they are favorable to the exclusion of any religious symbol from school property. For them, *laïcité* is defined substantively as a constraining value which guides their actions. In this category there are more teachers, who have been socialized solely in state schools and are often detached from religion. Indeed some are atheists, for whom school was a tool for social promotion. In the conflict over the veil they demanded a law prohibiting the wearing of religious symbols in state schools. They assimilate *laïcité* to the ideal of the Third Republic. This position can be interpreted as a defensive reflex to the crises and ongoing changes in the education system that is in the process of massification and subject to economic criteria for efficiency (for an analysis on the crisis of the concept of *laïcité* in parallel to that of the Republican school, see Dubet, 1996).

However, there are teachers acting according to rationality by finality and developing an ethic of responsibility. The manifestation of religion inside school shocks them but they are ready to define ways of compromising. In the conflict over the wearing of the headscarf, they refuse to expel the veiled students, preferring a long-term acculturation through the education system rather than an exclusion that would send the veiled young girls back to their family and community environment. These individuals are more often the school principals or the directors of secular associations or teachers' unions. Sometimes they hold religious beliefs. They attended alternatively state or private school and came from higher social and professional backgrounds. For them, *laïcité* is a procedural principle (in accordance with the procedural theories of justice of John Rawls and Jürgen Habermas, see Leclerc, 2001), a rule of the game that is negotiable within certain limits, namely in respect of human rights. They are favorable to managing conflicts over the veil on a case-by-case basis and claim a certain margin of action when adapting the rule. They take into account the diverse reasons for wearing the veil, rather than those that are exclusively religious (for example: the transitory aspect of the wearing of the veil such as an adolescence crisis, uneasiness regarding representations of the body and protection from a sexist environment in their neighborhood).

This pragmatic and open attitude is difficult to maintain in the context of the identity crisis of public schools and their teachers. Confronted with globalization, a large proportion of French leaders and public opinion reassert French political culture: the so-called 'French social model', public services *à la française*, and 'cultural exception'. In the same movement of self-defense, many of them support a strict *laïcité*, ignoring jurisprudential evolutions and local regulations that occurred or were enacted in France during the last twenty years. During the parliamentary Commission Stasi (2003), French media introduced a bias in the way they reported national debates on the wearing of religious symbols in schools. They gave space to disputes over the general principles rather than examining day to day local negotiations. They gave coverage to some local and strident headscarves disputes rather than reporting complex and ordinary compromises.

The law of March 15$^{th}$, 2004, forbidding the wearing of headscarves in public school, seems to be symptomatic of a reassertion of French political culture. In fact, when we examine the recent events which prompted the enacting of this law, *laïcité*, as part of French political culture, is not the explanatory variable as such, but rather bares a certain relationship to time and a particular way from which a collective entity produces its self-understanding. In times of crisis, a certain idealization of the past occurs. Developments that were the result of historical compromises and innovations are taken out of their original context, deprived of their historical complexity and became symbols of collective identity. What has been lost is the consciousness of how *laïcité* became a solution to national conflicts, while becoming a value of the social contract. This topic was examined by Jean Baubérot with his concept of *pacte laïque*. What has also been lost is the link between action and values, giving an impression of a static and rigid posture or political culture. *Laïcité* is perceived as a part of political culture when it is in crisis and no longer provides a workable framework of action connecting local conflicts and arrangements to national values. The concept of political culture is retrospective; this is what limits its explanatory dimension. It is an idealized vision of the past, a stereotypical self-definition, where values are no longer a model of action, an explanation of the present and a vision of the future.

## Conclusion: towards a negotiated and pedagogical *laïcité*

*Laïcité* appears to be a complex aspect of political culture, both in debates as well as in its continuous transformation. Many teachers, who are confronted with student demands for religious expression, used to make concessions between their secular values and the necessity to hold the classroom and integrate new arrivals. Between 1999 and 2000, when I studied the micro sociological interaction between teachers and students in secondary schools in the suburbs of Paris, I observed a diversity of conduct and the frequent adapting of strategies where the teachers put their personal secular beliefs to one side and where the students learned to formulate their observance of religious traditions in terms of individual rights and personal choices. Can this 'do-it-yourself'-attitude lead to overall changes in the political culture?

Looking back at recent evolutions, it must be acknowledged that the gathering of local situations and functional agreements between secular rule and the religious prescriptions of students have not led in return to a global change in the meaning of *laïcité* and more generally French political culture. This symbolic 're-codification' of reality was only partially achieved and imperfectly distributed. Local practice did not develop into a general vision of the new situation leading to the formulation of renewed principles. In the late 1990s, I observed, on the one hand, a disconnection between common sense, media constructions and the political analysis of veil affairs, and on the other hand, the complexity of the field. Both pieces of the jigsaw remain separated.

What was occurring in French *banlieues* has too often being perceived as an external problem, whereas it is a crisis of the integration system. Descendants of immigrants are also actors in the national collective history. The October 2005 riots were a forceful wake-up call. The focus, central in this volume, on the national political culture of a host country corrects the current reasoning that too often attributes the difficulties of their integration to new arrivals themselves. This is especially evident when blame is attached based on the assertion that Islamic faith is incompatible with western values. Integration has to be conceived as a process of interaction between the cultures of the host country and those of the immigrants. The challenge is to define a minimum of shared understanding and of shared methods and values, in order to resolve problems. A 'negotiated *laïcité'* is needed. A change in the political culture requires a diffusion of field work and comparative studies. Unfortunately, the century following the enactment of the 1905 law proved largely consensual and retrospective rather than prospective. It would appear that the rich vein of international academic debate and research on *laïcité* has not reached the general public. However, in the vision of Condorcet and Jules Ferry, *laïcité*, and more generally democratic politics, have always been a matter of long term pedagogy.

## References


Almond, G.A. & Verba, S. (1989). *The civic culture: Attitudes and democracy in five nations*. Newbury Park, Ca: Sage (original work published 1963.

Aubert, V. (1984). Système professionnel et esprit de corps: Le rôle du Syndicat ational des Instituteurs. *Pouvoirs, 30*, 79-89.

Aubert, V., Ozouf, J. & Ozouf, M. (1987). La tradition politique des instituteurs. *Pouvoirs, 42*, 53-65.

Barbier, M. (1995). *La Laïcité*. Paris: L'Harmattan.

Baubérot, J. (1990). *Vers un nouveau pacte laïque?* Paris: Seuil.

Baubérot, J. (1996). L'affaire des foulards. *L'Homme et la Société, 120*(2), 9-16.

Baubérot, J. (1999). Laïcité, sectes, société. In F. Champion & M. Cohen (eds.), *Sectes et démocratie* (pp. 315-317). Paris: Seuil.

Baubérot, J. (2004). *Laïcité (1905-2005), entre passion et raison*. Paris: Seuil.

Baudouin, J. & Portier, Ph. (2001). La laïcité française: Approche d'une métamorphose. In J. Baudouin & Ph. Portier (eds.), *La laïcité, une valeur d'aujourd'hui? Contestations et renégociations du modèle français* (pp. 15-34). Rennes: Presses Universitaires de Rennes.

Bianconi, A. (1987). *L'idéologie du Syndicat National des Instituteurs de 1929 à 1939*. Toulouse: Presses de l'Institut d'Etudes politiques de Toulouse.

Brubaker, R. (1992). *Citizenship and nationhood in France and Germany*. Cambridge: Harvard University Press.

Dubet, F. (1996). La Laïcité dans les mutations de l'école. In M.

Wieviorka & F. Dubet (eds.), *Une société fragmentée? Le multiculturalisme en débat* (pp. 85-112). Paris: La découverte/Poche Essais.

Gauchet, M. (1998). *La religion dans la démocratie: Parcours de la laïcité*. Paris: Le Débat, Gallimard.

Geertz, C. (1973). *The interpretation of cultures*. New York: Basic Books.

Guénifi-Souilamas, N. & Macé, E. (2006). *Les Féministes et le garçon arabe*. Paris: l'Aube, Poche Essai.

Leclerc, A. (2001). La contribution de la théorie procédurale de John Rawls à la redéfinition de la laïcité. In J. Baudouin & Ph. Portier (eds.), *La laïcité, une valeur d'aujourd'hui?Contestations et renégociations du modèle français* (pp. 229-246). Rennes: Presses Universitaires de Rennes.

Massignon, B. (2000). Laïcité et gestion de la diversité religieuse à l'école publique en France. *Social Compass, 47*(3), 353-366.

Molokotos-Liederman, L. (2000), Religious diversity in schools: The Muslim headscarf controversy and beyond. *Social Compass, 47*(3), 367-381.

Nicolet, Cl. (1982). *L'idée républicaine en France*. Paris, Gallimard.

Ognier, P. (2001). La laïcité française: Une histoire complexe et tourmentée. In B. Decouleurs et al., *La laïcité a-t-elle perdu la raison? L'enseignement sur les religions à l'école* (pp. 35-52). Paris: Parole et Silence.

Poulat, E. (1987). *Liberté, Laïcité: La guerre des deux France et le principe de modernité*. Paris: Cerf/Cujas.

Schemeil, Y. (1983). Les cultures politiques. In M. Grawitz & J. Léca (eds.), *Traité de Sciences politiques, T.III, « L'action politique »* (pp. 237-307). Paris: PUF.

Tribalat, M. (1995). *Faire France: Enquête sur les immigrés et leurs enfants*. Paris: La Découvertes/Essais.

Wieviorka, M. (1996). Introduction: Un débat nécessaire. In M. Wieviorka & F. Dubet (eds.), *Une société fragmentée? Le multiculturalisme en débat* (pp. 5-60). Paris: La découverte/Poche Essais.

Willaime, J.-P. (1990). Etat, éthique et religion. *Cahiers Internationaux de Sociologie, 88*, 189-213.

## Dutch way of dealing with religious difference

Peter van Rooden

### Introduction

The history of the Netherlands offers a rich field for analyzing concepts dealing with the relation between religion, religious groups, and political authority. There are two main reasons for this. In the first place, since their emergence as an independent political entity in the 1570s, the Northern Netherlands have been characterized by religious pluralism. Next to the state sponsored Reformed church, Mennonites, Catholics, Lutherans, Jews, and Arminians set up their own organizations and held their own religious services. Secondly, the political management of this religious diversity underwent marked changes over time. Any kind of Whig interpretation of these changes fails. Dutch religious history cannot be adequately interpreted as the development of toleration or the growth of religious liberty (see Hsia & Van Nierop (eds.), 2001). Huge shifts that have taken place in the way the Netherlands have dealt with religious difference.

I want to illustrate these difficulties by analyzing the concepts used over time to express religious difference. To analyze the way the relations between the various religious groups and political authority have been conceptualized over time, I have looked fairly systematically at legal texts (collected by De Visser, 1926-1927). Next to these legal sources, I have looked, much more loosely, at the way the various religious groups described themselves and others. The main conclusions to be drawn are threefold.

1. There have been indeed different periods marked by different ways of conceptualizing the relation between religious bodies and political authority in Dutch history. It is probably not justified to speak about different 'discourses', however. Charles Taylor's concept of 'social imaginaries' (Taylor, 2002) might be a better term, as,

2. in no period a clear-cut terminology to express its characteristic way of conceptualizing religious bodies existed. Even in the legal texts of the nineteenth century, supposedly produced by rational bureaucracies, we meet, sometimes within a single law, with widely different terms to denote the same phenomenon. What we deal with are not so much concepts, but common understandings, shared by large groups of people,

which do not primarily exist in theoretical or abstract form, yet enable social practices and confer a sense of legitimacy, precisely what Taylor considers social imaginaries to be. Consequently,

3. in the different Dutch social imaginaries of religious difference, the nature of the body politic always plays an overwhelmingly important role.

These social imaginaries of religion were always an integral part of the social practices, which gave them their meaning. The following argument does not rest simply on discourse analysis. Knowledge of the actual way religious diversity has been managed in the Netherlands over time is necessary to understand the meaning of the terms used to express religious diversity. In the following, I will, all too briefly, describe the different periods that I propose to distinguish, constructing their social imaginaries of religion, briefly discussing the terms used, and linking these with the prevailing nature of the body politic.

## Reformation (1572 – 1579)

During the Dutch Revolt, political opposition to the authority of the Habsburgs and the introduction of the Reformation became intertwined, clashing and reinforcing each other (Parker, 1977; Israel, 1995). The leader of the revolt, William of Orange, desperately tried to keep together his motley coalition of cities, estates, and nobles, only some of which wanted to introduce the Reformation. Attempts to evade the divisive potential of the religious question always involved proposals for a religious peace, which would allow 'the public exercise' of both the reformed and catholic 'religions' (De Visser, 1926-1927, pp. 155-156; Spaans, 2001). What was at issue was exactly this. The religious question concerned the public presence of religion, the institutional and liturgical aspects of Christianity. In these negotiations 'religion' did not mean a group of persons, or a separate organization, but the religious part of the politically controlled public sphere. In the course of the revolt, all attempts to divide this religious public sphere between Catholics and Protestants failed. Even so, the Union of Utrecht of 1579, the treaty which established what would become the Dutch Republic, allowed for the Estates of each province joining it to determine for themselves the kind of religion which would be 'publically exercised' (De Visser, pp. 170-176). In fact, all provinces joining the Union upheld the Reformed religion. The word *religie* in Dutch had been traditionally used to mark just this external, visible aspect of what we would call religion, being used, for instance, for 'religious duties', or the different practices of the religious orders.

Article 13 of the Union of Utrecht added that "every particular person will be allowed to be free in his religion, and no-one may be searched or inquired for the sake of religion". In these years, this meant no more than 'no Inquisition', but soon, already in the early seventeenth century, this principle was called 'freedom of conscience'. Right after the Synod of Dordrecht, in 1619, when the Arminians were repressed, it was extended to the private household, where families, if there were no strangers present, were allowed to 'read, sing or admonish' (*voorleesen, singen of vermanen*). This was explained as 'freedom of conscience or of particular feelings' (De Visser, 1926-1927, p. 244). No word was used making clear that what these people would be doing while 'singing, admonishing or reading' was religious.

The social imaginary of the social place of religion of the reformation years rested upon the notion that religion was part of a politically controlled public order. Conflicts concerned the nature of this order. The rule that people would not be persecuted for their personal beliefs and private conduct actually strengthened the notion that religion is predominantly embedded within a public order. The reformation period ended with an established Reformed church, recognized by a political entity which was highly decentralized, and had no clear locus of sovereignty.

## Confessional state (1579 – ca 1750)

The highly fragmented and politically decentralized nature of the Dutch Republic opened up spaces for the organization of dissident religious groups. This did not happen everywhere. In some parts of the Republic the political reformation took the form which was usual in the German Empire and led to confessional homogeneity. In several areas in the core of the Republic, however, both in the countryside and the cities, organized groups of religious dissenters emerged. Lutheran and Jewish communities were mainly the result of immigration. Although Catholic communities were strengthened by immigration too, they were mainly, like the Mennonites and Arminians, indigenous. Conflicts about the amount of liberty such groups were to be allowed played themselves out in different local setting and had different results (for a nice, late example Spaans, 2004). Still, by the last quarter of the seventeenth century the religiously mixed areas of the Dutch Republic had converged onto a similar pattern. Dissident religious groups had become part of the patronage networks by means of which the political authority of local elites was exercised. Their communities were governed by laymen, took care of their own poor, and were circumscribed by well-defined borders (Spaans, 2001). They also occupied a lower social space, symbolically expressed by their less visible church building, which were not allowed to intrude upon public space. Only the immigrant communities of Jews and Lutherans in Amsterdam could build magnificent churches and synagogues, which are still landmarks in the Amsterdam cityscape, even if they are today mainly used for different purposes.

The social imaginary of this religiously mixed society rested upon the contrast between a Reformed public order and various tolerated dissident groups. At the *Great Meeting*, the convocation of the different Estates of the United Provinces in 1651, convened to make sense of the Dutch Republic when the Eighty-Years War had ended, this social imaginary was perfectly expressed. The Estates decided, on the one hand, that all provinces would "maintain and preserve the true Christian Reformed Religion, as this today is preached and taught in the public churches of these countries...", and on the other that all "sects and denominations (*gezindheden*), which are secluded from public protection and whose existence is simply connived at (*geconniveert*), will be kept in all good order and quit" (De Visser, 1926-1927, pp. 280-304). Note that this declaration opposes a publicly taught religion to different groups, an opposition which rests upon different applications of political power. There is no overarching concept to describe what the Reformed and the dissenters might have in common. In general, in official discourse, the different dissenters are sometimes described as 'sects' or 'denominations' (*gezindheden'*) but more usual as members of their particular group. Catholics are called '*Papists'*, '*de Paepsgezinde deser landen', 'roomsgezinden', 'personen van de paepsche godsdienst'*, '*personen van de roomse gesintheyt'* (persuasion), '*roomsgezinde ingezeten'*, '*de rooms-catholieke ingezeten'*. In a similar way Mennonites could be called 'all those who are of the feeling or persuasion of the Mennonites' (*alle degene die van 't gevoelen ofte gesintheyt der mennoniten sijn ), 'menno gehesinde'*, '*mennonieten'*. The Jews are 'those of the Jewish Nation', while the Lutherans are 'those of the Augsburg confession' or mostly simply 'Lutherans'. All of these groups could thus be referred to by terms which made for a different mark of respect: 'Anabaptists' versus 'Mennonites', or 'Papists' versus 'Roman-Catholics inhabitants'. Arminians and Mennonites referred to themselves as a brotherhood or society, not claiming to be a church.

The main contrast here is with the Reformed, the members of the public church. They are hardly ever defined as a group. Even in the – fundamental – rule that dissenters were excluded from the exercise of political power, what was actually forbidden was the membership of a sect. The one reference to the Reformed as a group that I stumbled across, was a plea by the Estates of Zeeland for a stricter repression of the dissenters, because this would strengthen the allegiance of 'all true patriots' (De Visser, 1926-1927, p. 281). There did emerge, in the course of the seventeenth century, a notion of 'God's people' (*Gods volk*), but this was a term used by more or less radical pietists within the public church, to define the truly pious over against other Reformed, not to distinguish between Reformed and others.

The word 'Church' (*Kerk*) was quite common in the seventeenth and eighteenth centuries, yet it was not used to distinguish between different religious groups. It was always part of the social imaginary of the political community. The expression *Staat en Kerke*, 'State and Church' denotes the political and religious order of society, which stands over the subjects of the Republic. The Republic is depicted as a disciplined society. Its authorities uphold a public order, which has a political and an ecclesiastical aspect. 'Church' is used to denote the latter aspect of this public order (Van Rooden, 1999a). This early modern Dutch social imaginary of religion opposed a public religious order to various dissenting groups, and did not find it necessary to employ a single concept to denote what we might think that this order and these dissenting groups had in common. This social imaginary made it possible, both for contemporaries and present-day observers, to describe the religious order of the Dutch Republic as an instance of the early modern confessional state as well as an example of 'toleration' (Van Rooden, 2001). Even Reformed ministers could live with the existence of Mennonites or Catholics, provided they were kept in their place. Conversely, Mennonites and Arminians could praise the Dutch Republic because it left individuals free to pursue their own religious interests.

The notion of the Dutch Republic as defined by a public order led to a spate of historical writing. Religious histories mainly focused on the Synod of Dordrecht of 1618-1619, which was considered to be the basis of the religious order of the Republic (Van Rooden, 1998).

## Enlightenment and Revolution (ca 1750 – 1815)

The main change in the social imaginary of religion in the Netherlands took place within this period. For the first time, terms like 'religions' (*godsdiensten*) or 'churches' (*kerken*) emerged which made it possible to subsume the public church and the various dissenting bodies under overarching concepts, and to describe them as doing similar things. Ideologically, in terms of the history of ideas, this shift can be described as a confluence of pietist, Enlightened and republican currents. In the last half of the eighteenth century, the conceptual relation between political authority and citizens on the one hand, and public religion and piety on the other hand, changed decisively. The concepts were fused. Political authority was no longer depicted as a hierarchy, upholding order, but as an instance fostering a moral community of virtuous citizens. Religion was considered to be a force which created moral selves, committed to the public good. The new political and religious imaginaries could easily be integrated. The virtuous citizen is a pious believer, and religion is the source of the civic virtue which makes any nation strong. Accordingly, magistrates and ministers were no longer above all required to represent and uphold a public order. They had to foster moral selves committed to the national community. The contribution of other religious groups to this endeavor could be recognized (Van Rooden, 2004a).

This new cultural and religious nationalism — every citizen has to be a moral person, because he is a member of the national community, and this morality presupposes personal piety — was fostered from the late 1750s onwards by part of the political elite, by different groups which were instances of a new, enlightened sociability, and by enlightened and pietist currents within both the public church and the tolerated religious groups. It was deeply determined by the perceived decline of the Dutch Republic from its seventeenth century great power status. During the Seven-Years War, the Republic had been a very minor player indeed. Till the late 1770s, the new nationalism was markedly apolitical, in the fundamental sense that it did not lead to conflict. The catastrophic defeat which the Dutch Republic suffered in the Fourth English War (1780-84) led to a sudden political use of the new religious nationalism. Clearly, the defeat of the Dutch state was due to it not being a virtuous republic, a defect for which the government could be held accountable. The subsequent piecemeal democratic revolution, which developed very slowly, precisely because there was no clear centre in the Dutch Republic, was suppressed by Prussian troops in 1787. Eight years later, invading French revolutionary armies re-installed the defeated revolutionaries, who embarked on a radical overhaul of the Dutch state, in close dependence on French examples and support. They separated church and state, centralized the Dutch republic, and set up a strong central bureaucracy (Schama, 1977).

The social imaginary of religion and politics which made possible and legitimized these revolutionary acts had been prepared since the 1750s. Religion was no longer located in a religious order, but only in individuals, making all religious groups, including the public church, alike. Even conservative opponents of the revolution spoke, after their victory in 1787, about 'the true reformed religion (*godsdienst*)', opposing it to the 'tolerated religions (*godsdiensten*)' (De Visser, 1926-1927. p. 4). The Enlightened novels of Wolff and Deken of the 1780s had already used the word 'church' (*kerk*) to characterize both the public, and the dissenting churches. Reformed ministers in the late 1770s had taken care to point out to imagined audiences of dissenters that their church, too, was inculcating piety and creating virtuous citizens. Within this new social imaginary, the main forces working against true religion were intolerance, especially the intolerance of an established church which fostered hypocrisy by rewarding a shallow outward conformity, and superstition, defined as a lack of education, resulting in a slavish following of imposed conceptions and rituals (Van Rooden, 1999a). During the revolutionary period, this social imaginary made the separation of church and state possible. Everyone agreed that religion, in general, was the source of individual piety and thus of civic virtue. That was why no particular church ought to be privileged by political authority.

If we look at the terms used to legislate religion in the rapidly following different constitutions between 1795 and 1816 (there were six of them), including their different drafts, we find a bewildering variety of concepts (De Visser, 1926-1927). The principle of the separation of church and state could be expressed as 'there will no longer be a privileged or established church in the Netherlands', but also as 'the separation of religion (*godsdienst*) from the state', or as the disestablishment of the 'established religion' (*heersende godsdienst*) . It might also be formulated as 'the church is separated from the state, and the confession of any religion (*godsdienst*) does not entail any civil advantages or disadvantages'. In this formulation, religion could also be described as 'ecclesiastical doctrine'. Although occasionally it seems clear that the use of certain terms indicates allegiance to particular politico-religious currents, in general one has to say that this terminological confusion was the result of the problem of having to express a new social imaginary in legal language. The new imaginary distinguished between (1) the essence of religion (inculcating personal piety and virtue), (2) the social organizations by which piety and virtue were inculcated, and (3) the doctrinal and liturgical aspects which distinguished these social organizations from one another. The term 'religion' (*godsdienst*) could be used for all or each of these three aspects. The social aspect could also be expressed by the terms 'church' (*kerk*), 'ecclesiastical society' (*kerkgenootschap*), 'religious society' (*godsdienstig genootschap*), 'religious community' (*godsdienstige gemeenschap*), or 'denomination' (*gezindheid*). No discourse here, or a profitable mine for *Begriffsgeschichte*. As this disturbingly confusing terminology makes clear, the origin of the new Dutch social imaginary of religion is not to be found in a single theory, philosophy, or ideological current. It was the result of the practices of the Dutch confessional state before 1750, which had integrated all religious organizations into the local political bodies, of the Enlightened interpretation of the international decline of the Dutch Republic as a consequence of the loss of ancestral virtue, and the wide penetration of pietistic conceptions in eighteenth century Dutch religious life.

In the period leading up to 1795 and during the radical phase of the Batavian Republic, till 1801, the opposition of true religion to intolerance and superstition was turned mainly against the former public church, although even during this period there was a persistent undercurrent of a modern form of anti-Catholicism, focusing on the supposed backwardness and moral degradation of this religion (Clemens, 1995). When the Batavian Republic, following its French masters, took a right-wing turn after 1801, anti-Catholicism became much stronger. In 1806, the new constitution, following the French law of 1802 'relative a l'organisation des cultes', allowed the government to regulate the organization and exercise of all cults (*erediensten*; French: *cultes*) (De Visser, 1926-1927, pp. 93-94).

In the two centuries following the revolutionary period, quite radical changes in the social place of religion have taken place in the Netherlands, yet the constitutional development of church-state relations stayed within the range of the various terms laid down around 1800. The huge changes in the actual position of organized Christian groups within Dutch society of the nineteenth and twentieth century were hardly reflected in formal legal concepts. During the revolutionary period a social imaginary of religious bodies as organizations of religious and moral selves had become established. During the last two centuries, the Kingdom of the Netherlands has thrown up different social constellations which can be based upon this fundamental social imaginary. These different constellations were not reflected in legal concepts, but at best in vernacular discourses, which are much harder to reconstruct.

## Protestant nation (1815 – 1888)

After the fall of Napoleon the Netherlands were reorganized as a Kingdom, which included the former Austrian Netherlands, present-day Belgium. The new Kingdom was highly authoritarian and centralized, taking over the centralized bureaucracy built up during the revolutionary years. It exercised its revolutionary powers to the full, using the law of 1806 to restructure all Protestant groups in the North so that they would become nation-building organizations. Its heavy-handed attempt to do the same with the Catholic Church was one of the main factors driving the Belgians to revolt in 1830. The various constitutions of the new kingdom show the same terminological confusion which had characterized the revolutionary years. Religious bodies are called 'religions' (*godsdiensten*), 'churches' (*kerken*), 'denominations' (*gezindheden*, but also *gezindten*) and 'ecclesiastical societies '(*kerkgenootschappen*).

The social imaginary of religion in these years is still basically that of the revolutionary years, primarily because the new Kingdom of the Netherlands imagined its subjects as members of a moral community as well. Yet the social imaginary had drifted significantly to the right. The members of this moral community need to be educated and morally informed, a task which can only be undertaken by nationally organized bodies which are recognized by the government. The moral community of the nation is something which has to be produced, and which might be broken by actions of uninformed common people, or of foreign-directed Catholic priests. The former public church was now often called the national or patriotic (*vaderlandse*) church, even when the former Protestant dissenters were assimilated to it, their ministers being educated at the same universities, their prominent laymen becoming part of the political elite. The new Kingdom celebrated the centenary of the Reformation (in 1817), instead of that of the Synod of Dordrecht (in 1819). In general, the newly emerging historical genre of church history described Dutch religious history as the growth of the nation (Van Rooden, 1999b).

This new celebration of Protestantism (a term which only became common in the nineteenth century) also justified the way in which the Dutch state treated the overwhelming mass of its subjects not as citizens, but as objects to be improved and transformed. The nation is a moral community, yet only a small part of the citizens are truly moral selves. Religion was the most important means by which this educational relation between the state and its subjects was expressed. The legitimation of political inequality was based as much upon practice as upon ideology. During the first three quarters of the nineteenth century, the Dutch Protestant churches, supported by the state-sponsored primary education system, engaged in an unprecedented process of religious education, which raised religious knowledge all around, even as it confirmed the processes of cultural class-formation which formed the basis of the new Dutch nation state. The main others of this social imaginary were lower-class secessionists of the former public church, claiming to be truly Reformed, and, of course, Catholics, which made up some 35% of the population of the Netherlands after the revolt of Belgium. In general discourse, the opposition between 'roomsen' and 'Dutch' seems to have been the most important.

Political conflicts within this period focused on authoritarianism, the extent to which the executive was to be able to get its way. The liberal victory of 1848 loosened the links between religious bodies and the state. The new constitution (still using the same old mish-mash of terms) eased life for the lower-class dissenters and made possible the reintroduction of a Catholic episcopal hierarchy in the Netherlands, an event which was opposed by one of the largest mass-movements in Dutch history (Vis & Janse (eds.), 2002). Yet this liberal loosening of control did not involve a rejection of the notion of the 'Protestant nation'. It was just a fight about how to achieve this. The political and social imaginary remained that of a single moral community of individual citizens, committed to each other and to the nation. Implicitly, this nation was still considered to be Protestant. An opposition between Protestants and Catholics, even when not expressed in legal or political terms, was always implied by this social imaginary. The recognized Protestant churches were seen as the main mechanisms by which citizens were produced. In these years, a historical lexicon offering short biographies of ministers, could be called 'The Protestant nation' (*het protestantse vaderland*), expressing quite nicely the educationalist and elitists aspects of this notion of Protestantism (Langeraad & Visscher, 1903-1918).

### The pillarized society (1888 – ca 1966)

With the introduction of mass-politics in the Netherlands in the last quarter of the nineteenth century, this elitist Protestant version of the modern social imaginary of religion was broken. Abraham Kuyper, a minister who was also a stunningly capable mass-politician, split the Protestants. He led a right-wing secession from the former public church and created the first modern mass-political party in the Netherlands. His main attraction to his (mainly lower class) followers was his claim that they were not lacking in knowledge, but had preserved it. They still upheld Calvinist (a new term, introduced by Kuyper) doctrine, while the upper levels of church and state had been usurped by liberals. This notion radically subverted the educational paternalism on which the nineteenth century Dutch state had rested. Kuyper's second claim was that the Dutch nation had always been made up from three different *gezindheden*, liberal-humanists, Calvinists and Catholics, currents which he described both as persuasions and as groups (Van Rooden, 1996, pp. 185-190).

This notion of the Dutch nation as made up, not of individuals who were to be educated into members of the moral community of the nation, but of different groups characterized by their peculiar religious convictions, justified the political alliance between orthodox Protestants and Catholics. From 1889 onwards, this coalition managed to win about half of all elections. After the introduction of general suffrage, in 1917, the absolute majority of the coalition was assured till the mid 1960s.

The political power which was acquired in this way was used to build up staggering dense and complex social worlds, starting with separate educational systems but spilling over, eventually, in almost all aspects of social life: you would be a member of Catholic trade-union, play table tennis as a Catholic, breed goats as a Catholic, live in a house build by a Catholic state-subsidized corporation, use fertilizer provided by a Catholic farmers' organization. The same went for the orthodox Protestants.

This huge shift in the social place of religion in the Netherlands happened without any notable change in the legal and political terms used to denote churches. A commission set up in the early 1920s to review the several laws concerning religion clearly did not like the term 'ecclesiastical societies' (*kerkgenootschappen*) which had become the most common concept to denote religious bodies, because it seemed to imply that churches were like secular societies (which they are not in Dutch law). Yet they did not want to use the term 'churches', because the concept 'church' might lead to theological controversies between Protestants and Catholics. All laws set up to make possible the social expansion of the Protestant and Catholic movements, for instance those regarding education, avoided references to religion as far as possible. In general, in Dutch society in the twentieth century, the existence of very strong religious minority movements within society, who together held an absolute majority, yet defined themselves over against each other, and has led to a very secularized public sphere. To denote themselves, the religious/social groups used terms defining themselves as groups made up of individuals: 'we, Roman-Catholics', 'we, Calvinists' or 'we, anti-Revolutionaries'. The different sections could be described as *volksgroepen* or *volksdelen.* The social imaginary had shifted decisively. The Dutch nation was still considered to be made up of individuals, but these individuals were thought to belong to different groups, and their allegiance to the nation could only be expressed by means of the membership of these groups. In effect, religion had become ethnicized (Van Rooden, 1996, pp. 169-199).

As was the case with the emergence of the modern social imaginary in the mid-eighteenth century, this new view of the place of religion in Dutch society had been prepared by earlier social practices. The educational drive of the nineteenth century Dutch state and churches had produced the possibility of religious mobilization amongst the Protestants once mass-politics were introduced. Its persistent anti-Catholicism had laid the basis for religious-political Catholic mobilization. The split amongst the Protestants ensured that the ghetto-builders would form a clear majority.

The new social imaginary and its practices were fiercely contested. Kuyper was truly hated for breaking up the unity of the nation and delivering it to Rome (Van Rooden, 1997). After the Second World War, when there was a common surge for renewal, the former public church allied itself with the new welfare state and, though less explicitly, with the Socialists, which had shed their German orientation and looked instead towards the modernizing British Labour Party. In a dizzying surge of renewal, it enthusiastically embraced social engineering by the state and modern American management techniques as a way to overcome the inefficiency and non-Christian character of the divisions within Dutch society (Ruitenberg, 1956; Van der Linde, 1995). Its not-so-secret hope was to put the Catholics and neo-Calvinists in their place. Theologians of the former public church involved with this movement coined the term *verzuiling*, pillarization, which has become the standard social science concept to describe Dutch society in the twentieth century.

**Dechristianization and the coming of Islam (ca 1966 – 2000)**

It was not the reorganization of the former public church which ended the period of pillarization. The orthodox Protestants and Catholics had spoken to their members as if they were the disenfranchised. After half a century of Christian Democratic political rule, and the tremendous social upward mobility of their members, this conceptual strategy did not reflect any social reality. The modern Dutch welfare state, build up in the 1960s, broke the hold of the religious organizations over their members. Most importantly, the cultural revolution of the 1960s, with its stress on consumption and individual self-fulfillment clashed radically with the unreflexive and authoritarian character of the religious practices of pillarized Dutch Christianity (Van Rooden, 2004b). As public discourse had become secularized during the twentieth century, the new version of the modern social imaginary of the Netherlands did not involve religion at all. The Netherlands were considered to be made up of individuals, who were tolerant of each other's choices as expressed in their consumption and life-styles. It was probably the very success of the pillarized movements to define religion as a total commitment to a group which made it impossible for the Dutch churches to thrive in this new environment. People still define organized religion as something which imposes a total social identity, which they do not desire.

In the last quarter of the twentieth century, large numbers of Muslims emigrated to the Netherlands (Rath et al., 1996). They find themselves in a strange situation. On the one hand, legal opportunities to organize themselves religiously and as a subculture abound. The legal framework which made pillarization possible is still in place. On the other hand, they are quite often used as the Other to express the new social imaginary of a nation of tolerant individuals. They are interpreted as an instance of the religious past which the Dutch have discarded. In a recent speech, a Dutch cabinet minister explained to Muslim clerics that precisely because Dutch society is tolerant, they had to change their ways and religion. In a mirror image of the ideal of the expressive self, toleration is considered to have to do mainly with questions of gender, especially the acceptance of homosexuality and female emancipation.

The present-day attitude towards Muslims is an almost perfect parallel to the way in which the nineteenth-century Kingdom approached the Catholics. The Catholics were, ultimately, integrated into the Dutch nation by pillarization. Yet this mechanism does not seem to be viable for Muslims. The success of pillarization rested upon the existence of several ideological groups, who together organized a majority of the population. The combination of legal structures making it easy to organize yourself as a subculture, persistent views of the Muslim as the Other of the myriad individual life style projects which the Dutch are supposed to have embraced, and the contemporary world-wide Islamic revival, seem to make it highly probable that Muslims in the Netherlands will become a clearly marked minority.

## Concluding remarks

Religion, in the history of the Netherlands, always has been the main boundary marker between different groups, and the historical process of Dutch state formation always has exercised tremendous influence on the way these boundaries were upheld. Yet the nature of the conflicts and of the public space in which they were resolved, as well as the solutions adopted to deal with them, show huge differences. They cannot be subsumed under a single master-narrative, describing the Dutch way of dealing with religious difference.

The concept of political culture is used in the introduction of this book to draw attention to the way in which the treatment of religious newcomers is determined by long-term characteristics of the nation-states where they settle. Yet it seems doubtful that the concept can help circumvent the radical discontinuity which characterizes the Dutch history of dealing with religious difference. There is a long-standing interpretation of Dutch political life as essentially a rule by committee, averse to authoritarian or violent policies, and skewed towards compromise, negotiation, and inclusion. This political style would have characterized the exercise of political authority in the Netherlands since the days of the *regenten*, the magistrates of the cities of the Dutch Republic. Quite apart from the question whether this is an accurate description of the nature of political authority during the Dutch Republic, this description of Dutch political culture seems too thin and shallow to offer rich contributions to historical understanding. A tendency towards compromise and negotiation can easily lead to the exclusion of those who are supposed not to know the rules and whose requests or wishes therefore need not to be taken seriously. Even a political culture of compromise and inclusion can change decisively, when the ground rules defining legitimate difference change.

Assume for a moment that the mass immigration from Turkey and North Africa to the Netherlands had taken place in the 1950s. The new immigrants would immediately have been considered to be a religious, and not a cultural group. Their traditional sexual morals could not have become a marker of difference. This religious difference might have led to popular prejudices and discrimination, yet the political system and culture was well geared to deal with such problems. Muslims would not have been considered subjects to be transformed, before they could be accepted, but as a community whose leaders would have to learn the Dutch way of reaching compromise. Muslims as a group would not have become the Other of Dutch identity. In the 1990s, however, while the culture of compromise and toleration was still in place, the practical meaning of this culture had changed decisively. What had to be tolerated, and about what subjects compromise could be reached, was no longer the same.

I would plea for a much shorter time span to analyze and explain the reactions of nation states towards religious newcomers. The slow but inexorable dying of Dutch Christianity since the 1960s is much more important for understanding contemporary reactions to Muslims than the practical multi-culturalism of the pillarized society, let alone the religious regimes of the Dutch Republic or the early nineteenth-century Kingdom of the Netherlands.

The opposition between secular and religious definitions of the nation state does not seem to be so fundamental as argued in the introduction. Secular definitions have strong religious consequences. The Dutch Protestant nation of the nineteenth century proudly proclaimed its tolerant virtue and its upholding of religious freedom, yet these secular achievements simultaneously kept the Dutch Catholics in their place. The dechristianized Dutch nation at the beginning of the twenty-first century does not find it at all easy to deal with religious difference. Secular definitions of the nation are not by definition better, or more tolerant. Dutch religious history is a perfect illustration that there is no 'solution' to the problem of religious difference: there are just different ways of managing diversity and living together, some better, some worse.

## References


Clemens, T. (1995). De terugdringing van de rooms-katholieken uit de verlicht-protestantse natie. *Bijdragen en mededelingen betreffende de geschiedenis der Nederlanden, 110*(1), 27-39.

De Visser, J.Th. (1926-1927) *Kerk en staat.* Leiden: Sijthoff.

Hsia, R.P. & Van Nierop, H. (eds.). (2001). *Calvinism and religious toleration in the Dutch Golden Age.* Cambridge: Cambridge University Press.

Israel, J. (1995). *The Dutch republic: Its rise, greatness, and fall 1477-1806.* Oxford: Clarendon Press.

Parker, G. (1977). *The Dutch revolt.* London: Allen Lane.

Rath, J. et al. (1996). *Nederland en zijn Islam: Een ontzuilende samenleving reageert op het ontstaan van een geloofsgemeenschap.* Amsterdam: Het Spinhuis.

Ruitenberg, L.H. (ed.). (1956). *Verklaringen, kanselafkondigingen, boodschappen, herderlijke brieven en rapporten, uitgevaardigd door of namens de Generale Synode der Nederlandse Hervormde Kerk in de jaren 1945-1955.* Den Haag: Boekencentrum.

Schama, S. (1977). *Patriots and liberators: Revolution in the Netherlands 1780-1813.* London: Collins.

Spaans, J. (2001). Religious policies in the seventeenth century Dutch Republic. In R.P. Hsia & H. van Nierop (eds.), *Calvinism and religious toleration in the Dutch Golden Age* (pp. 72-86). Cambridge: Cambridge University Press,.

Spaans, J. (2004). De luthersche lobby voor vrijheid van godsdienstoefening in Friesland. *De Zeventiende Eeuw, 20*(1), 38-52.

Taylor, Ch. (2002). Modern social imaginaries. *Public Culture, 14*(1), 91-125.

Van der Linde, J.M. (1995). *Werkelijk, ik kan alles: Werkers in kerkelijke arbeid in de Nederlandse hervormde kerk, 1945-1966.* Zoetermeer: Boekencentrum.

Van Langeraad, L.A. & Visscher, H. (1903-1918) *Het protestantsche vaderland.* Utrecht: Kemink.

Van Rooden, P. (1996). *Religieuze regimes: Over godsdienst en maatschappij in Nederland 1570-1990.* Amsterdam: Bert Bakker.

Van Rooden, P. (1997). Kuyper en Hoedemaker over de volkskerk. *Kerktijd, 9*(3), 30-38.

Van Rooden, P. (1998). Dutch Protestantism and its pasts. In R. Swanson (ed.), *The church retrospective* (pp. 254-263). Woodbridge: Boydell Press.

Van Rooden, P. (1999a). Godsdienst en nationalisme in de vroeg-moderne tijd: Het voorbeeld van de Republiek. In N. van Sas (ed.), *Vaderland: Een begripsgeschiedenis* (pp. 201-236). Amsterdam: Amsterdam University Press.

Van Rooden, P. (1999b). History, the nation and religion: The transformations of the Dutch religious past. In H. Lehmann & P. van de Veer (eds.), *Nation and religion Perspectives on Europe and* Asia (pp. 96-111). Princeton: Princeton University Press.

Van Rooden, P. (2001) The Jews and religious toleration in the Dutch Republic. In R.P. Hsia & H. van Nierop (eds.), *Calvinism and religious toleration in the Dutch Golden Age* (pp. 132-147). Cambridge: Cambridge University Press.

Van Rooden, P. (2004) Public orders into moral communities: Eighteenth-century fast and thanksgiving day sermons in the Dutch Republic and New England. In K. Cooper & J. Gregory (eds.), *Retribution, reconciliation and repentance* (pp. 218-239). Woodbridge: Boydell Press.

Van Rooden, P. (2004b). Oral history en het vreemde sterven van het Nederlands christendom. *Bijdragen en mededelingen betreffende de geschiedenis der Nederlanden, 119*(4), 524-551.

Vis, J. & Janse, W. (eds.). (2002). *Staf en storm: Het herstel van de bisschoppelijke hiërarchie in Nederland in 1853: actie en reactie.* Hilversum: Verloren.

# Part 2: religious minorities in the Dutch and French nation state

# Dutch and Catholic

## The Catholic Church and Dutch Catholics in the Dutch nation state since 1795

Erik Sengers

### Introduction

The central issue of this volume about the reaction of different nations to religious newcomers seems rather irrelevant when speaking about Catholics in the Netherlands, even though the subject provides an interesting example of the interaction between a religious group and the nation state it inhabits. This 'irrelevance' would seem to be double: Firstly, because the Catholic (or Latin-rite) Church is not a religious newcomer to the modern Dutch state in the strict sense of the word. The Church has been present in the Netherlands since the 7th century, when the Franks built a small church in what is now the city of Utrecht, which has been an episcopal see ever since. The Church had enormous political, cultural and social influence during the middle ages, until the Protestant reformation brought an end to it. As a result, the Church went underground and only reappeared in the public sphere after the invasion of the French revolutionary troops (1795), when it was allowed to do so (see Van Eijnatten & Van Lieburg, 2005). In this sense, therefore, the Catholic Church *can* be seen as a religious newcomer. Secondly, the issue seems irrelevant because the principles and framework of the liberal, pluralistic and yet national Dutch state have not changed much from 1800 to the present day, especially in the sphere of the relationship between state and Church(es). The Batavian government, inspired by the French Revolution and backed by French troops, declared religious freedom and equality for all Churches in 1796. This principle was reformulated in the liberal constitution of 1848 and expanded to all religions and world-views in the constitution of 1983. In this context, therefore, the state did not really have a particular reaction to the Catholic Church as a 'newcomer', although the demands of the Church in the public domain posed a serious challenge to its status quo in the 19th and 20th centuries.

When considering the Catholic Church and Dutch Catholics as religious newcomers in the modern, national Dutch state, a more complicated question emerges. Traditionally, the Catholic Church is considered to be an anomaly in the Dutch nation state, by non-Catholic citizens, by scholars of Dutch religious history, and by Catholics themselves. The myths of the Dutch nation state are strongly connected to the historical events of the war of national liberation, from 1568 to 1648. As a result of this war, the Reformed Church became the public church in the United Provinces and shaped Dutch mentality for centuries. Moreover, the rise of the protestant House of Orange to the Dutch throne after 1813 reasserted the cultural and political status of Protestantism in Dutch society. Catholics seemed to play a secondary role in the nation state, not only according to external opinion, but also according to their own self-understanding. Due to the relative stability of the political framework, the dynamic between the Catholic Church and the nation state should therefore be interpreted primarily as the reaction of the Church and Catholics to the way the modern nation state developed (see e.g. Hellemans, 1990), rather than the reaction of the nation state to the Catholic Church. That dynamic was an attempt to come to terms with their double identity as Catholics and Dutchmen. The conflicts between Church and state in the 19th century should – from this perspective – be seen as an ongoing discussion about how constitutional freedom should be interpreted and what it implied. As Catholics were not the only 'religious newcomers' in this period, the Dutch state was challenged to expand its liberal framework to all these religious groups – a struggle that resulted in a nation state that was built on a multiplicity of religious identities.

The thesis I present in this article is that the integration of Catholics in the Dutch nation state was brought about primarily by internal changes within Catholic subculture, and I will demonstrate this thesis by analyzing the history of the relationship of Dutch Catholicism with the nation state in three periods: from 1795-1870 (a period of remarkable participation), the central period of 1870-1960 (during which the Church initially opposed the nation state, although later becoming incorporated), and the post-1960 decades (during which the formation of the state was concluded and developed into a welfare state, with new consequences for the Catholic Church). Furthermore, my aim is to show that it was Catholics themselves who willingly and knowingly adapted to the nation state, albeit recognizing the immense difficulty they must have experienced in coming to terms with the seducing forces of modernity that came with it. In the conclusion, I will compare the history of the relationship of the Dutch Catholic Church with the nation state to the present-day position of Islam in Dutch society.

## 1795-1870: Participation in a new state

*The state: liberal and united*

A new period in Dutch history began when the French revolutionary troops attacked and finally occupied the Dutch Republic in 1795. The National Assembly of the Batavian Republic quickly accepted the declaration of human rights, recognizing all citizens as equal before the law and installing universal suffrage for male citizens. Major changes in the religious sphere were enacted: the power of the state-favored Reformed Church was weakened by the obligation of civil marriage, the abolition of the restrictions on inter-confessional marriages and the withdrawal of public schools from the supervision of the Reformed Church (De Wit, 1983). Other measures promoted equality between the diverse religious organizations: the favored position of the Reformed Church was abolished in 1796 and church-buildings had to be distributed fairly among the denominations.

The new regime offered unprecedented possibilities to the Catholic Church. Catholics were now allowed to found seminaries for the education of the clergy, to construct new church buildings and to install parishes. But it was freedom and equality *under* the law: since religion was supposed to provide social peace, it had to be under the supervision of the state. To prevent religious strife, all religious symbols were banned from the public sphere. In the Napoleonic regime, churches in the Netherlands were also subjected to strict state control. A Ministry for Catholic Cult severely limited freedom of religion, and the King (during 1806-1810 Napoleon's brother, Louis) acquired the right to intervene in the inner life of the churches (De Jong, 1998, pp. 212-213, 219-221). After the annexation of the Netherlands by France (1810), the 'extinction decrees' aimed at abolishing religious orders also came into force.

The liberated Dutch Kingdom of 1813 continued most of these measures initiated during the French period (Bornewasser, 1981, p. 169). Equality of the churches was guaranteed, and they were provided with funding by the government. Funding for poor relief was also provided, and schools were incorporated into the state (De Jong, 1998, pp. 205, 227-228, 234). Any expression of religion in the public sphere remained forbidden, and the extinction measures pertaining to religious orders remained in force until 1840, although charitable orders were tolerated. Concerned about the revolutionary situation in Europe in 1848, King William II ordered a liberal constitution to be written. Although the text itself did not imply great change for the constitutional position of the churches, the implications of other articles in this constitution were enormous, especially for the Catholic Church. Freedom of speech, press, association and religion (Boogman, 1977) offered unprecedented possibilities of expanding Catholic influence, as these were no longer under state control. In 1853 however, religious freedom was once again limited, with the law on church-organizations, which was especially written to limit the influence of the Catholic Church in the public sphere (Schokking, 1894, pp. 300-352). This law was in force until 1983, but was never very effective.

*Catholic citizens*

Even before 1795, Catholics had profited from the trend towards liberalization in the 18th century Dutch Republic. Under the influence of the Enlightenment, provincial governments were willing to offer Catholics a better position in politics and society (Clemens, 1995, p. 29). For their part, Catholics worked energetically for the recognition of their position as Christians and citizens, emphasizing and drawing attention to their patriotism with regard to the Dutch nation. Moreover, they did not hesitate to use Enlightenment reasoning in their struggle. A wide-ranging ecumenical debate emerged, in which Catholics eagerly sought to demonstrate that their faith and its dogmas were in line with reason. They even published some treatises on the reformation of the Church according to the principles of the Enlightenment (Bornewasser, 1987). In this way Catholics participated in the broader cultural context of the prerevolutionary Dutch Republic.

Catholics and other (religious) dissenters welcomed the political change of 1795, expecting it to bring about an improvement of their position in the state and society. It is therefore not surprising that they played an important role in the revolution of 1795. According to Rogier, almost all Catholics were in favor of the new regime and in general played a leading role in the patriotic movement (Rogier & De Rooy, 1953, p. 21). They were involved in requests to the new government for more democracy, were members of civil committees and the burgher militias, published political treatises and led local revolts and revolutionary assemblies. Even some priests were found amongst the revolutionary ranks. In the National Assembly, Catholics defended national unity, patriotism and the values of the Enlightenment (Roosendaal, 1993, pp. 271-276). This liberal, national and enlightened attitude prevailed within the Catholic subculture until the mid 19th century, above all in politics, where the Catholic faction in parliament supported the liberals in their attempt to modernize society. A manifesto written to stimulate Catholic support of the Liberals was very well received among their fellow believers. The liberal-Catholics controlled the 'Catholic group' in Parliament up until 1871, when more clericalist ('ultramontane') groups took over.

*Catholic identity*

Beyond these movements, developments internal and external to the Church led to a more distinct position of the Church in Dutch society. Now and then, Catholics clashed with the Enlightenment culture and thought as used by the liberal-protestant elites to keep Catholics out of politics (Clemens, 1995, pp. 31-38). The Church also clashed with the state when it forcefully tried to control the Church; for example, during the negotiations for a concordat (where the King, against the will of the Church, upheld his right to appoint bishops), with regard to the ban on public processions and over the state-controlled seminary that candidates for the priesthood had to attend. When in 1853 the episcopal structure was reinstalled, social conflicts between Catholics and Protestants broke out, the latter of whom saw the appointment of bishops as an attack on Dutch identity and history and were afraid that a foreign power (the Papacy) would meddle in Dutch politics (Bronkhorst, 1953, pp. 32-68). The widespread harassment of Catholics and assaults on priests showed that, despite formal equality, Catholics were still not socially accepted.

But a separate Catholic identity was also fostered by internal factors. After the fall of Napoleon, the Roman Curia sought to re-establish the Church's political leverage in European politics. As a consequence, the Church sharply repudiated Enlightenment ideas, and turned her back on the modern notions of rationalism, democracy, tolerance and the civil freedom of religion, of speech and that of the press (Bornewasser, 1989). Moreover, some Dutch Catholics promoted a distinct Catholic identity in the new nation-state. Catholic lay-intellectuals like Le Sage ten Broek, Alberdingk Thijm and Nuyens, as well as the expanding Catholic press, promoted the study of the history of Dutch Catholicism, seeking to connect it to the canonical history of the Dutch nation (thereby correcting the largely protestant canon), and encouraged their fellow-Catholics to participate in national politics, culture and science – as *Roman* Catholics (Versluis, 1948, pp. 31-37, 157-162; Rogier & De Rooy, 1953, pp. 278-279; Peijnenburg, 1976, pp. 44-60). Neo-gothic art and architecture were used to highlight and build continuity between the medieval, united Dutch society and the modern Dutch nation, as well as to give a distinct identity to the Dutch Catholics in society.

The liberalization of Dutch society presented an opportunity to rebuild the Church. Seminaries were reopened and religious orders and congregations were founded. In 1853, Rome reinstalled the Catholic hierarchy that had been absent since the 17$^{th}$ century. Bishops quickly arranged their dioceses and reorganized the chaotic parish structure (Rogier & De Rooy, 1953, pp. 200-210; Van Laarhoven, 1965). The Liberals, however, did not want to go much further than this, and they viewed the upsurge of Catholic activities with some misgivings. Liberals were inclined to underline the secular concept of the state and society, whereas Catholics wanted to grasp this opportunity to put their own stamp on Dutch society, politics and culture. The two issues that triggered the fiercest and most enduring conflicts between the Catholic Church and the (liberal) state were education and charity. According to the 1848 constitution poor relief was a 'concern' of the government, but as they had not done much about it, in reality it was a private (mostly church-based) affair. After 1851, however, the government wanted to reassert its leadership in this field. Bishops, however, regarded such state control as a violation of the freedom of religion and reacted defensively, attempting to bring all poor relief under Church control (Van Loo, 1987, pp. 47-48, 108-109).

According to the bishops, freedom of religion was also at stake in the school issue. The Constitution granted the right to found denominational schools. But as the government improved the public schools and imposed these measures also on the private ones without giving them the financial support necessary to enable them to conform to the new legislation, bishops felt their constitutional freedom was limited. In 1869 they circulated an *ex cathedra* statement that forbade Catholics to send their children to state schools and stimulated the founding of Catholic schools (De Wolf, 1983). These two issues caused a break between liberals and Catholics in 1871. The Church withdrew, and for almost a century assumed a defensive position with regard to the state, demanding the right to exercise her constitutional freedom in all aspects of life (Bronkhorst, 1953, pp. 105-111).

## 1870-1960: Conflict and cooperation

*Development of a nation-state*

The French united the Low Countries, but it was not until after 1870 that various legal and technical developments gave birth to a distinct Dutch nation-state. Coherence between the different areas of the country was increased by improvements in the infrastructure. Telegraph (1852) and telephone (1888), together with media such as the press, film, radio (1919) and television (1930), created a nation-wide communication structure. The unity of the Dutch society was further boosted by a national vocabulary (1883), the standardization of grammar (1896) and the introduction of a standard time for the whole country (1909). Finally, the connection of citizens across the nation to national politics was enhanced by the introduction of a proportional electoral system (1917) and the expansion of the suffrage to every citizen (1922) (Knippenberg & De Pater, 1988, pp. 19, 31, 40, 52-86, 137).

Culturally, the Dutch people evolved into a more tightly knit national community. The inauguration of Queen Wilhelmina (1898) boosted sentiments of nationalism and monarchism. A new generation of artists painted and promoted Dutch landscapes. Commemorations of great Dutchmen, such as Rembrandt, imbued new generations of children with patriotic feelings, and the 17$^{th}$ century was now glorified as the 'Golden Age' of Dutch history. The building of the *Vredespaleis* ('Peace Palace') in The Hague gave the Dutch the image of being guardians of world peace (Bank & Van Buuren, 2000, pp. 21-88). But other factors also created a kind of 'national' culture. Urbanization promoted the rise of an urban mass culture (Bank & Van Buuren, pp. 523-566). The new industrial and urban society promoted equality among citizens and softened class differences and privileges. The introduction of national standards in the educational system also promoted unity and equality among new generations. However, this new unity was threatened by fresh divisions along religious and socio-political lines (pillarization and the rise of socialism, respectively).

*The Church: separation and defence*

Catholic bishops initially reacted against this greater unity with a call for separation. They saw the modern nation state as a threat to Catholic unity and values, and therefore to the very identification of Catholics with their Church. As noted above, in 1870 bishops formally instructed Catholics to enroll their children in Catholic schools. On the eve of the elections of 1933, bishops warned against modern political ideas and forbade Catholics to enter non-Catholic social and political societies, especially socialist ones. Another letter in 1934 warned against the national-socialist groups which, like the social democrats, held certain attraction for some Catholics. As late as 1954, bishops threatened with excommunication those Catholics who would become members of non-Catholic organizations. The policy of these bishops was very successful: research on the late 1950's shows that most Catholics participated only in Catholic organizations (Sengers, 2003a, pp. 92-94). The unity and group-identity of Catholics in society was encouraged in other ways as well. Marriages between Catholics and non-Catholics were considered a major threat to the faith of the Catholic partner and, consequently, to the vitality of the Catholic subculture. Such so-called 'mixed marriages' were only permitted under the condition of severe obligations for the Catholic partner, among them the duty to convert the non-Catholic partner and to raise the children in the Catholic faith. This policy was also successful: between 1914 and 1960 the number of inter-religious marriages among all Catholic marriages declined from 13% to 4.5%. Public devotions such as pilgrimages and the canonization of Dutch saints, the Martyrs of Gorcum (1867), Peter Canisius (1864/1925) and Lydwina of Schiedam (1890), who were assumed to exemplify 'typical' Dutch characteristics, created a distinct Dutch-Catholic identity. On national Catholic feast-days, the unity and solidarity of Catholics and their organizations was ritually enacted and displayed to the nation at large (Van Xanten, 2007). Finally, the separate identity of Catholics was affirmed in the culture of everyday life, and this in various ways: Catholics had different first names, wore their wedding ring on their left hand, used a different vocabulary, and cultivated a different taste in furniture and other areas of taste and style (Sengers, pp. 97-100).

At the same time, the Church violently and aggressively attacked modern society. Several apologetic groups at the beginning of the 20th century tried to 'defend' the Church against attacks from non-believers, seeking to win over converts and to reunite other Churches with the Catholic 'Mother Church'. In the framework of Catholic Action, lay people were educated to be able to resist the 'evil' forces of modernity at home, in the neighborhood and in the workplace, as well as to convert non-Catholics and to stimulate the 'luke-warm' in their faith to greater activity. An initiative called 'For God' (1936) pursued the same ideals, seeking to encourage Catholic organizations to fight the ungodly, communism, the 'new heathens' (i.e. fascism), freemasonry and neo-

Malthusianism. A small initiative in Amsterdam even had the pretension of converting the whole city (Sengers, 2003a, pp. 94-95). In order to protect Catholics against dangerous ideas, the Church sought to keep them away from the mass media. Modern literature was seen as evil and the List of Prohibited Books (the famous *Index*, edited in Rome) decided what Catholics could and could not read. Organizations in the Netherlands and Catholic libraries informed Catholics about this list and promoted the 'good' book. A censor was established that controlled Catholic newspapers, and Catholics were warned not to read non-Catholic newspapers. To supervise the consumption of movies by Catholics, a Catholic Film Office rated movies according to Catholic morals (Sengers, pp. 96-97).

This aggressive stance of the Catholic Church against the modern nation-state and its demands for freedom and self-determination fanned the flames of latent anti-Catholic feelings in Dutch society. Combined with the growth of the Catholic population, these demands were seen as a threat to Dutch national identity and the freedom of Dutch society. The passionate veneration of Catholics for the pope (De Valk, 1998, pp. 134-143, 157-172; Rogier & De Rooy, 1953, pp. 206, 265-266), who was seen by Protestants and liberals alike as a foreign potentate, showed that Catholics were not to be trusted, or were even potential traitors. On the other hand, the temporary withdrawal of the Dutch consulate from the Holy See (1871) made it clear to Catholics that they had not been accepted as full citizens, and restrictions imposed on Catholic processions were seen as a severe limitation of their constitutional freedom (Van Zuthem, [2001]). These measures caused fierce debates in the Dutch parliament (De Valk, 1998, pp. 211-234). Mutual distrust and tension were fuelled on the occasion of the beatification of Carolus Borromeaus (1910), when Protestants were vilified as materialistic, worldly enemies of Christ Even after the Second World War, this bad feeling of Protestants towards Catholicism had not disappeared (Rogier & De Rooy, 1953, pp. 688, 811-814): the Reformed Synod of 1950 warned against the sub-cultural isolation of the Catholics, their growing political influence and their insistence on the unique authority of the Roman Catholic Church.

*Integration after 1920*

Despite its propensity to self-isolation (as discussed above), the Catholic Church was gradually integrated into Dutch society and politics from1920 onwards. Various factors lead to this integration. First, the position of the Church towards society and politics changed. The papal encyclical letter Rerum Novarum (1891) stimulated Catholics all over the world to not withdraw from society but to seriously concern themselves with social problems, to find solutions to them and to engage in national politics. Several Catholic historical journals sought to rediscover the Dutch-Catholic national identity, and on the centennial of Dutch independence from France (1913), Catholics published a beautiful two-volume book that showed the positive contributions of Catholics to Dutch society during the century that had elapsed since 1813. After the silver jubilee of King William III (1874), bishops had stimulated Catholics to participate in national festivities and since the inauguration of Queen Wilhelmina (1898) Catholics were strongly oriented towards supporting the monarchy (Groot, 2000).

From the state's perspective, a vast number of Catholic social organizations were subsidized by the government and therefore had to comply with national legal and administrative rules for their funding (Pennings, 1991, pp. 145-149). Moreover, those organizations aimed at assisting Catholics to become decent and useful members of Dutch society. Tensions with the state eased after 1870, when the Ministry for Catholic Cult was finally abolished, thus putting an end to state supervision of the internal business of the Church. After the introduction of universal suffrage and proportional representation in 1917/1922, Catholics became the largest party in Parliament. In many subsequent governments it was from their ranks that the prime minister came. Finally, the attitude of Catholics towards other Churches and religions changed from emphasizing differences to underlining common Christian principles and common problems in an increasingly secularized society (Jacobs, 1998).

Furthermore, the numerous Catholic social organizations present across the nation furthered the participation of Catholics in broader Dutch society. Youth organizations not only improved the professional skills of young workers, but also taught them how to be good and loyal employees, decent fathers and mothers, and loyal citizens of the state, thus providing a framework for a larger participation of Dutch Catholics in society. Specialized organizations fought alcoholism and its harmful social and physical consequences (Heikens, 1985, pp. 45-68). In addition to this, the social position of Catholics was improved by the rise of specialized welfare and health care. Catholics were being cared for in Catholic hospitals, Catholic nursery homes and Catholic institutions for mental and psychiatric care and oriented by Catholic offices for advice on marriage and upbringing (Duffhues et al., 1985, pp. 83-98, 102-114). The participation of Catholics was also stimulated by the growing Catholic school sector. Catholics were initially reluctant to enter secondary schools because of their presumed rationalistic character. But after a fierce political struggle, in coalition with the Protestant Anti-Revolutionary Party, the government cleared the way for the founding of denominational secondary schools financed by the state. Catholic secondary schools were founded all over the country and the participation of Catholics in secondary schools grew to a level comparable to their relative number in Dutch society (Matthijssen, 1958, pp. 72-84). Finally, Catholics even founded their own Catholic university which, again with public funding, was meant to build a bridge between the Dutch Catholic subculture and general Dutch society.

As a consequence of these developments, increasing numbers of Catholics attained an equal position in the labor market as their non-Catholic colleagues. They began to occupy higher positions in firms and businesses. The number of Catholics in academic positions and professions also grew steadily in the first half of the 20th century. With their social organizations that separated them from, and at the same time integrated them into, the broader national culture, Catholics (together with Protestants) reshaped the nation into a distinct Christian and pillarized society (Lijphart, [1975]), and in this way secured their position in the culture and politics of the nation state.

## After 1960: Welfare state and Catholic Church

*From nation-state to welfare state*

Dutch state and nation-building in the Netherlands was more or less concluded by 1960. However, there have been two significant changes in Dutch society and its political system since then that have caused a reaction by the Catholic Church towards society and the state. The first was the rise of the welfare state. Made possible by the growth of the economy, new social laws guaranteed financial support in all situations possible: child allowance (1963), health insurance (1964), social security (1965), disability insurance (1967) and the minimum wage (1968). As well as this, more public funding was transferred to welfare organizations that professionalized their assistance, which at the same time, and because of this funding, came under a stronger control of the local government (Luiten van Zanden, 1997, pp. 81-100). The school sector in particular, was reorganized so that women and lower social groups could more easily enter and enjoy secondary and higher education.

The second profound change was the secularization and ever-increasing diversity of Dutch society, on many levels. Workers demanded a voice in the management of firms (Gout, 1982). The position of women improved, not least because of their own efforts, but also due to economic and political changes. Both as a result of their improved education and economic necessity women participated more in the labor market, and in 1971 were declared equals in marriage. A distinct youth culture arose that contested the overriding 'consumer society', western bourgeois values and, last but not the least, the war in Vietnam. In the course of these social changes and the protest movements they gave rise to, a more liberal and individualistic ethos began to pervade Dutch society. Sexual morality was liberalized, in tandem with a broad move towards a more permissive society. A good example of this new trend was the protracted conflict about abortion that was finally terminated when Parliament passed a very liberal law, in accordance with international standards (Gout, 1982, pp. 356-360). In the 1990's euthanasia was partially legalized, and changing views on the family together with a more tolerant attitude towards homosexual relationships led firstly to the partnership contract, and then to the legalization of gay marriages.

Immigration further fragmented the religious landscape. Muslims, Hindus and other religious groups entered a society that had traditionally been Christian with Jewish and Humanistic minorities. Relations between the state and the mainstream Christian Churches became steadily more tenuous and the social and political influence of the Christian Churches declined as they came (and were seen) to represent less than half of the Dutch population.

*The assimilation of Catholicism in Dutch society*

In line with the growing integration of the Catholic Church in the Dutch state in the former period, the Church was at this stage almost completely assimilated into modern Dutch society and wholeheartedly accepted the national state. Catholics had now begun to view themselves as normal Dutch citizens, and considered their organizations and religious traditions as part and parcel of Dutch society. Consequently, they put less emphasis on their distinct position in society.

After the Second Vatican Council, the Church accepted the basic principles of human rights and those of modern western society. The Church also engaged more in social issues, speaking publicly about them and frequently taking the side of the poor and the powerless (Sengers, 2003a, pp. 153-154). The old divisions in the religious field were relativized, as the Dutch Catholic Church recognized the Protestant Churches as being partners in Christ and wholeheartedly supported the ecumenical movement, as well as inter-religious dialogue with the Jewish community (Sengers, pp. 158-161). However, in the late 1980's, a reaction set in, partly caused by a conservative turn in Rome after the death of John XXIII. Dutch bishops sought to re-emphasize the Church's distinct calling in society, in particular by combating secularism and the permissive trend in sexual morality (Sengers, pp. 163-179, 2003b). However, this conservative policy remained largely ineffectual, both within the Catholic community and in Dutch society as a whole.

By far the most visible change in the presence of the Catholic Church in Dutch society was the dismantling of the vast network of Catholic social organizations. In 1954, Catholics had been called upon to enter only Catholic organizations, but already in 1960, bishops accepted and even encouraged Catholics to follow their own conscience in becoming members of organizations of their own choice, whether these were Catholic or not. Thereafter, the entire social fabric of the Catholic subculture speedily disintegrated: the Catholic Labor Union merged with the socialist one, the Catholic People's Party merged into a broader Christian-Democratic party (1980), Catholic libraries became members of the public library organization, and Catholic welfare work with youngsters was completely taken over by the state. Under economic pressure, the Catholic press cast off its Catholic identity and sought to attract new readers with a progressive and secularized profile. Catholic schools no longer advertised their confessional identity: the organizational ties with the Church were largely severed, and teachers were no longer obliged to be active member of the Church (Sengers, 2003a, pp. 156-158). As the other Christian pillars, especially the neo-Calvinist one (Dekker, 1992), were secularized and/or disintegrated as well, religion and religious diversity were no longer as central as before to the image of the Dutch nation.

## Conclusion

The relationship between Catholics, the Catholic Church and the modern Dutch Nation State has been profoundly transformed during the 19th and 20th century, as can be seen in the analysis above. It is interesting to note that it was not the state that took the initiative in this process of change – the general framework of the modern, liberal, pluralistic and national Dutch state remained stable in the modern period. Rather, it was the Catholic Church itself that changed its position towards the state and the nation.

In the first phase, Catholics, silently tolerated by their leaders, engaged in politics, culture and society after the French invasion, and then later within the new kingdom. At the same time, Catholic bishops, under the influence of ultramontanism, slowed down this process of integration, mobilizing Catholics against the modern state, and seeking to put their own Catholic stamp on Dutch culture and society. In a second period, the Church initially took an aggressive position against modern society and the nation state, demanding the freedom to organize its internal life according to its own, religiously based principles. Paradoxically, as the state accepted and responded to its demands, the Church became more and more integrated into the Dutch state, society and culture. In the last period, the Church completely abolished its distinct and separate position, and bishops themselves agreed to dissolve the Catholic subculture and organizational structure, being wholeheartedly assimilated into Dutch society. The main result of this mobilization of Catholics (and other religious minorities) was that the definition of the liberal, pluralistic, national state was expanded so that these groups, through the organization of a pillarized society, could find their place in it. The influence of the state in this respect was not visible and overt, but silent and covert, through funding and financial commissioning, while always holding firmly to the liberal principles of the Dutch state.

The history of the interaction between Catholics and the Catholic Church with the nation state and their fellow citizens, portrays some aspects which are typical of Dutch political culture. The neutral, liberal and secular nation state that was set up after 1815 was never pushed through to its final consequences – although there were some tendencies to do just this. Religious pluriformity and the position of religious organizations in society were always accepted. As first and foremost pietist Calvinists and then Roman Catholics mobilized their followers to demand their 'right' place in Dutch society, politics, culture and historiography, the liberal conception of the state was adapted so that these groups could be integrated in it. The result was not so much the 'E pluribus unum' (one out of diversity), of the United States of America, but more an emphasis on religious diversity and de-emphasizing national unity. Some very strong, secular institutions such as the Royal House, the liberal constitution, parliamentary democracy and the law maintained the unity of the state, and it was here that Catholics and other religious and political minorities had to find a positive relationship with them, were they to be accepted as ordinary citizens by their fellow Dutchman. What was achieved is due to the merit of both Dutch Catholics and the non-Catholic Dutch elites: the former because managed to bring about this positive relationship with the state, and the latter for being able to re-interpret the concept of the Dutch nation state in a more pluralistic direction.

The presence of Islam in the Netherlands confronts Dutch society once again today with the task of integrating a religious minority into its political, social and cultural fabric. In this case also, things are seldom what they seem. Islam is, as Catholicism was, already present in Dutch society: firstly, Muslims participate in several areas of Dutch society as lawyers, prosecutors, businessmen, artists, civil servants, teachers and so forth. Secondly, Islam is seen, as Catholicism was before it, as being 'strange' and foreign to Dutch national culture and a 'threat' to Dutch values. In order to diminish this threat in the eyes of the Dutch, great pressure is exercised on Muslims, as it was on Catholics, to relativize the importance of their religion and culture, and to integrate into Dutch society. Finally, the discussion is once again about constitutional rights and in particular, the expansion of the Muslim school sector (Rath et al., 1996). With Islam, therefore, Dutch society is  not facing new questions, but old ones.

Despite this similarity, there is a major difference: today, it is far less clear what is being demanded by the hosting society. The Dutch state at present has (almost) nothing in common with the 19th century image of the nation state: it has largely broken off its roots with history, it has no clear 'national' set of values or cultural standards, it has no shared religion and no clear ethnic make-up. While Catholics in the late 19$^{th}$ and early 20$^{th}$ century were fully aware of the nature of the national culture that confronted them, it is not clear in what state or nation today's Muslims have to participate. The definite ethnic (though in reality ethnically diverse) and religious make-up of these new religious newcomers, combined with the general fear of Islamic terrorism since 9/11, are perceived as a threat to the secular, tolerant and liberal self-image of Dutch society and national identity. It is not a coincidence that the appearance of this religious newcomer has occasioned a new debate about the foundations of Dutch national identity (which has, of course, been spurred on by other developments as well, such as European integration and globalization; see Lechner, 2008). Examples of this debate can be found in the discussion about a 'national canon' in history, as well as the ongoing issue about Dutch 'norms and values' (De Beer & Den Hoed, 2004).

So the question to be faced, as seen from this perspective, is not so much how to integrate Islam into Dutch society, but rather whether the Dutch are able to (re)discover their constitutional freedom (of religion, speech, association and press), and whether they are willing to offer these to the religious newcomers? In order to do that they will have to expand and broaden their understanding of national identity and unity so that Muslims can be included in it. The alternative, and the question remains open as to whether it will be the one chosen, is to stick to a narrow, western, secular, ethnically Dutch concept of the nation. It is my considered opinion that the Dutch constitution, political traditions and national culture offer fair freedom and equality for every citizen. It is this framework that allowed Catholics, as well as other religious, ethnic and political groups, to participate in Dutch society and to integrate themselves into it without insurmountable problems. At present, Dutch Muslims, like the Catholics of the $19^{th}$ century, demand that these rights are granted to them as well. Denying them these rights would give the wrong signal and would, moreover, be a violation of the principles that constitute modern Dutch society.

## References

Bank, J. & Van Buuren, M. (2000). *1900: Hoogtij van burgerlijke cultuur*. Den Haag: SDU-uitgevers.

Boogman, J.C. (1977). De 'revolutie' van 1848 en haar nasleep. In H.F.J.M. van den Eerenbeemt et al. (eds.), *Algemene geschiedenis der Nederlanden XII* (pp. 333-352). Haarlem: Fibula-Van Dishoeck.

Bornewasser, J.A. (1981). The authority of the Dutch state over the churches 1795-1853. In A.C. Duke & C.A. Tamse (eds.), *Church and state since the Reformation* (pp. 154-175). Den Haag: Martinus Nijhoff.

Bornewasser, J.A. (1987). Inleiding. In F. Dröes & S. Verschuren (eds.), *Katholiek Nederland en de Verlichting: Een werkboek (Deel I)* (pp. 5-16). Tilburg: Theologische Faculteit Tilburg.

Bornewasser, J.A. (1989). *Katholieke kerk en Restauratie*. Tilburg: Tilburg University Press.

Bronkhorst, A.J. (1953). *Rondom 1853: De invoering der rooms-*

*katholieke hiërarchie, de April-beweging*. 's Gravenhage: Boekencentrum.
Clemens, Th. (1995). De terugdringing van de rooms-katholieken uit de Verlicht-protestantse natie. *Bijdragen en mededelingen tot de geschiedenis der Nederlanden, 110*(1), 27-39.
De Beer, P. & Den Hoed, P. (eds.) (2004). *Wat gij niet wilt dat u geschiedt...: Verkorte weergave van het WRR-rapport 'Waarden, normen en de last van het gedrag'*. Amsterdam: Amsterdam university press/Salomé.
De Jong, O.J. (1998). Uitkeringen aan de kerken. In J. de Bruyn et al. (eds.), *Geen heersende kerk,geen heersende staat. De verhouding tussen kerken en staat 1796-1996* (pp. 203-249). Zoetermeer: Meinema.
De Valk, J.P. (1998). *Roomser dan de Paus? Studies over de betrekkingen tussen de Heilige Stoel en het Nederlands katholicisme 1815-1840: Een wetenschappelijke proeve op het gebied van de letteren*. Nijmegen: Valkhof Pers.
De Wit, C.H.E. (1983). De Noordelijke Nederlanden in de Bataafse en Franse tijd 1795-1813. In H.F.J.M. van den Eerenbeemt et al. (eds.), *Algemene geschiedenis der Nederlanden XI* (pp. 158-186). Haarlem: Fibula-Van Dishoeck.
De Wolf, H.C. (1983). Onderwijs en opvoeding in de Noordelijke Nederlanden 1795-1813/Onderwijs en opvoeding in de Noordelijke Nederlanden 1813-circa 1840. In H.F.J.M. van den Eerenbeemt et al. (eds.), *Algemene geschiedenis der Nederlanden XI* (pp. 36-46/102-116). Haarlem: Fibula-Van Dishoeck.
Dekker, G. (1992). *De stille revolutie: De ontwikkeling van de Gereformeerde Kerken in Nederland tussen 1950 en 1990*. Kampen: J.H. Kok.
Duffhues, T. et al. (1985). *Bewegende patronen: Een analyse van het landelijk netwerk van katholieke organisaties en bestuurders 1945-1980*. Nijmegen-Baarn: KDC-Ambo.
Gout, F.P. (1982). Het socio-culturele leven in Nederland 1945-1980. In H.F.J.M. van Den Eerenbeemt et al. (eds.), *Algemene geschiedenis der Nederlanden XV* (pp. 337-368). Haarlem: Fibula-Van Dishoeck.
Groot, F. (2000). Vlaggen in top en stenen door de ruiten: De natie in de steigers 1850-1940. In J.H.C. Blom & J. Talsma (eds.), *De verzuiling voorbij: Godsdienst, stand en natie in de lange negentiende eeuw* (pp. 171-200). Amsterdam: Het Spinhuis.
Heikens, Tj. (1985). Onmaatschappelijkheidsbestrijding. In Tj.

Akkermans & S. Stuurman (eds.) *De zondige rivièra van het katholicisme: Een lokale studie over feminisme en ontzuiling 1950-1975* (pp. 38-73). Amsterdam: SUA.
Hellemans, S. (1990). *Strijd om de moderniteit: Sociale bewegingen en verzuiling in Europa sinds 1800*. Leuven: Universitaire Pers Leuven.
Jacobs, J. (1998). IJkpunt 1950: Het begin van een nieuwe bezinning, van isolement naar beginnende openheid. In C. Augustijn & E. Honée (eds.), *Vervreemding en verzoening. De relatie tussen katholieken en protestanten in Nederland 1550-2000* (pp. 151-170). Nijmegen: Valkhof Pers.
Knippenberg, H. & De Pater, B. (1988). *De eenwording van Nederland: Schaalvergroting en integratie sinds 1800*. Nijmegen: SUN.
Lechner, F. (2008). *The Netherlands. Globalization and national identity*. New York-Abingdon: Routledge/Taylor & Francis.
Lijphart, A. [1975]. *The politics of accommodation: Pluralism and democracy in the Netherlands*. Berkeley, etc.: University of California press.
Luiten van Zanden, J. (1997). *Een klein land in de 20^e eeuw: Economische geschiedenis van Nederland 1914-1945*. Utrecht: Het Spectrum.
Matthijssen, M. (1958) *De intellectuele emancipatie der katholieken: Historische en sociografische analyse van het Nederlands katholiek middelbaar onderwijs*. Assen: Van Gorcum/Hak & Prakke.
Peijnenburg, J.W.M. (1976). *Judocus Smits en zijn Tijd*. Amsterdam: De Tijd.
Pennings, P.J.M. (1991). *Verzuiling en ontzuiling - de lokale verschillen: Opbouw, instandhouding en neergang van plaatselijke zuilen in verschillende delen van Nederland na 1800*. Kampen: J.H. Kok.
Rath, J. et al. (1996). *Nederland en zijn Islam: Een ontzuilende samenleving reageert op het ontstaan van een geloofsgemeenschap*. Amsterdam: Het Spinhuis.
Rogier, L.J. & De Rooy, N. (1953). *In vrijheid herboren: Katholiek Nederland 1853-1953*. 's Gravenhage: Pax.
Roosendaal, J. (1993). Geloof en revolutie: De Nederlandse katholieken en het oecumenisch christen-radicalisme. In M. Monteiro et al. (eds.), *De dynamiek van religie en cultuur: Geschiedenis van het Nederlands katholicisme* (pp. 261-281). Kampen: Kok.
Schokking, J. (1894). *Historisch-juridische schets van de wet van de 10den september 1853, tot regeling van het toezicht op de*

*onderscheidende kerkgenootschappen*. Leiden: Daamen.
Sengers, E. (2003a). *"Al zijn we katholiek, we zijn Nederlanders": Opkomst en verval van de katholieke kerk in Nederland sinds 1795 vanuit rational-choice perspectief.* Delft: Eburon.
Sengers, E. (2003b). You don't have to be a saint or a practicing Catholic...: Higher tension and lower attachment in the Dutch Catholic Church since 1970. *Antonianum, 88*(3) 529-545.
Van Eijnatten, J. & Van Lieburg, F. (2005). *Nederlandse religiegeschiedenis*. Hilversum: Verloren.
Van Laarhoven, J.C.P. (1965). *Een kerkprovincie in concilie*. Utrecht-Nijmegen: Dekker & Van de Vegt.
Van Loo, L.F. (1987). *"Den arme gegeven...". Een beschrijving van armoede, armenzorg en sociale zekerheid in Nederland 1784-1965.* Amsterdam-Meppel: Boom (2nd impression).
Van Xanten, H.J. (2007). *'Katholieken, wat zijt gij toch een wonderlijk volk!'. De Katholiekendagen in Nederland 1899-1940*. Nijmegen: Valkhof Pers.
Van Zuthem, J. [2001]. *'Heelen en halven': Orthodox-protestantse voormannen en het 'politiek' antipapisme in de periode 1872-1925.* Hilversum: Verloren.
Versluis, W.G. (1948). *Geschiedenis van de emancipatie der katholieken in Nederland van 1795-heden*. Utrecht-Nijmegen: Dekker & Van de Vegt.

# Protestantism in France

## A minority defining its place in Catholic culture

Jean-Paul Willaime

### France: a Catholic country?

Although France remains an overwhelmingly Catholic country, it is much less so today than before. According to the European Values Surveys whereas 70% of French people declared themselves as Catholic in 1981, only 42% did so in 2008 (Bréchon & Tchernia, 2009, p. 229). This notable decline in the proportion of Catholics is accompanied by an increase in people who declare themselves as having 'no stated [religious] affiliation' (from 18% to 33% according to the same survey), and in those declaring themselves as 'confirmed atheists' (from 9% to 17%). In 2008 therefore, 50% of those surveyed in France either do not state a religion, or are 'confirmed atheists'. And although we observe an increase in the number of people saying they are of 'another religion' (from 3% to 8%), this is clearly due to the presence of a Muslim minority estimated to comprise 6.5% of the population, or around 4 million people.

In this context, where does the Protestant minority stand? Although the European Values Surveys do not provide specifics, other surveys have shown that Protestantism, while remaining very much a minority religion, still represents around 2% of the population, or about 1.5 million people out of 63 million living in France. Whereas the proportion of French people who identify with Catholicism has greatly declined, this is not the case with those French who identify with Protestantism. Not only does the Protestant minority maintain stable numbers, but it is also growing slightly, if we are to believe some surveys (at least those people declaring themselves as 'close to Protestantism', at 3%). In 1995, 3% of the French population (1.7 million people) declared themselves as 'close to Protestantism' in their answers to a poll asking them which religion they felt closest to. This percentage, which is higher than the officially recognized percentage of French Protestants, reveals that people outside of the Church community are sympathetic toward the Protestant microminority. This outside support helps strengthen French Protestantism. As many observers of the Protestant world have noted, this stability or this slight increase is mainly due to the development of evangelical or Pentecostal Protestantism which, although it is not a new phenomenon, has grown in size (to more than 400,000 believers), particularly, but not exclusively, among the West Indian, Romani and African communities in France.

The Protestant minority in France has therefore seen three great changes over the past few years. Firstly, the proportion of Protestants to Catholics is no longer 2% to 70%, but 2% to 42%. This is quite a change for a Christian minority that has often considered itself as being dominated by Roman Catholicism, very much the majority religion. Secondly, it is becoming much more diverse, both on a cultural level (with various 'ethnic churches') and on a religious level (the appearance of multifaceted evangelical and Pentecostal movements). Third, it leads to a stronger affirmation of the protestant identity in the framework of the French surrounding society, just as well towards the state as at the local level of the social life.

## Protestants in France

In France, Protestantism is often ignored or poorly understood. The Protestant religion's lack of visibility in society has something to do with this. But the often 'catholic-centered' image of Christianity in a country like France, where the majority of residents identify culturally with Catholicism, does not help matters. For example in the media, 'Christianity' and 'Roman Catholicism' are used interchangeably, and one refers to 'the Church' in the singular. The growing diversity of the Protestant world, offering a wide variety of Churches (from the most progressive to the most fundamentalist), adds another level of difficulty in understanding it. While it once had a relatively favorable public image among the French at a time when they knew only of its Reformed and Lutheran movements, doubts have grown following the development, in France as in other countries, of more militant and proselytizing forms of Protestantism involving conversions (the evangelical and Pentecostal Churches). In many ways, we can say that in French society, Protestantism is an active minority whose diversity can be seen in its numerous Churches, charities and movements.

Even though the Protestant reform movement has specifically French origins – which should not be underestimated, as John Calvin was born in France (in 1509, in the town of Noyon in Picardy) – and even though

Huguenots comprised around 10% of the Kingdom of France in the sixteenth century, the royal authorities extensively persecuted Protestants in the name of Catholicism, the state religion: first under Richelieu who destroyed Protestant political power (the fall of La Rochelle in 1628, the Peace of Alais in 1629), then especially under Louis XIV who in 1685 revoked the 1598 Edict of Nantes which had granted them some level of recognition within the Kingdom. For a century – from 1685 to the 1787 Edict of Toleration – Protestantism was outlawed in France, as a quarter of the 800,000 Protestants in France at that time (out of a population of 18 million) fled to other countries: Germany, England, the Netherlands, Switzerland, and even for some, America and South Africa. But the French Revolution and its consequences (the system of recognized religions that Napoleon put in place in 1802), followed by the Republic, finally granted definitive recognition to Protestants in French society. One can then understand why they sided with the social and political forces that fought for the separation of Church and State and the secularization of schools. In these areas, their role under the Third Republic (1870—1940) was particularly important. As minority, they support a state which freed from his privileged bonds with the Catholic Church and promote a secular school welcoming pupils from different religious and philosophical backgrounds. In this period, different protestant persons, as Ferdinand Buisson in the field of the school, were involved in the public sphere and the political life.

French Protestants have never forgotten the past persecutions and are quite concerned about the respect for religious and philosophical diversity. This was especially apparent in 1985, the 300th anniversary of the revocation of the edict of Nantes. Every year at the *Musée du désert*, located in Mialet in the *Gard* department, more than ten thousand Protestants gather to remember a particular chapter from their painful history, in order to draw conclusions for the present. There has also been an increase in the number of Protestant museums, as well as a constant level of activity by the *Société d'Histoire du Protestantisme Français* (founded in 1852), which publishes a quarterly journal, the *Bulletin de la Société d'Histoire du Protestantisme Français*, and organizes conferences. The Protestant minority in France cultivates its history and strives to keep the memory of the events that marked it alive.

French Protestants are represented in varying proportions throughout the country: while sparsely present in many areas (Brittany and the *Centre* region), they are more visible in others (Alsace, the *Gard* and *Ardèche* departments, and the area surrounding Montbéliard). As a result of the migration of Protestants from rural parts of France where the religion had traditionally become established to more urban zones, Protestantism is now most visible in the metropolitan areas of cities like Paris, Strasbourg, Marseille, Nîmes, Montpellier, and Mulhouse.

Traditionally, French Protestantism is mainly of the Reformed variety, in other words Calvinist, but it is principally Lutheran in the Alsace region and near Montbéliard. As signatories to the Leuenberg Agreement (1973) – which recognizes full communion between the Reformed and Lutheran Churches in Europe – the French branches of these churches have close relations: depending on their representation in each part of the country, followers can attend services either in a Lutheran or Reformed church. Many ministers willingly give services in churches of either branch. In addition, there is a *Permanent Lutheran-Reformed Council*, enabling the Lutheran and Reformed Churches in France to strengthen their ties: these churches are slowly becoming unified. But they do not account for all of French Protestantism: there are also Baptist, Methodist, Pentecostal, and various evangelical Churches, as well as Mennonite congregations, all of whom form minorities of their own within the Protestant minority, which is comprised mainly of the Lutheran and Reformed Churches.

The Protestant Federation of France (*Fédération Protestante de France* or F.P.F.) represents nearly all of French Protestantism; bringing together most of the Protestant churches and associations in France, it acts on their behalf at the governmental level and looks out for their common interests while contributing to mutual understanding between all of its members. Created in 1905, a month before the passage of the law separating Church and State, the F.P.F. held its first meeting in 1907, while the first plenary assembly took place in Nîmes in 1909. A charter, adopted in 1993, underlines the 'unity in diversity' of the F.P.F. members and specifies what F.P.F. membership is all about. The F.P.F. handles the chaplaincy program in the armed services for all of French Protestantism, and produces Protestant radio and television programs (like *Présence Protestante*, broadcast Sunday mornings on the *France 2* channel). There are 81 communities, institutions, charities and movements in all (Communities of Deaconesses; youth and adult movements; educational, health and social programs; various institutions), representing more than 500 associations belonging to the F.P.F., which comprises 22 Churches or Church Unions representing a total of 1400 parishes. 1650 ministers, including 200 women, serve one of the Churches belonging to the F.P.F.

The followers of the F.P.F.'s Churches or Church Unions can be divided into three main groupings: one third in Alsace and the *Moselle* department (the members of the *Union des Églises Protestants d'Alsace et de Lorraine* which is mainly Lutheran), one third for the Reformed Church of France (*l'Église Réformée de France*, whose roots are Calvinist) and one third in various evangelical Churches. Finally, there are in fact two distinct Churches in Alsace and Moselle: the Protestant Church of the Augsburg Confession and the Reformed Protestant Church. This is not due to church doctrine, but to the special history of this region. Unlike the rest of France where Church and State have been separated since 1905, the Churches in Alsace and Moselle, located in an area that was annexed to Germany from 1870 to 1918, still function under the system of recognized religions that was in place in France before 1905. In this region, the 1801 Concordat and the *Articles Organiques* of 1802 are still in force, which means among other things that Lutheran and Reformed ministers are employees of the state, as are Catholic priests and Jewish rabbis. Although some evangelical and Pentecostal Churches belong to the F.P.F., many others do not. The creation in 2002 and the institutionalization in 2010 of a National Council of French Evangelicals (*Conseil National des Evangéliques de France*) is proof of the vitality of the evangelical movement and its willingness to develop its own structures.

## Protestant contributions to French nation

French Protestantism, despite being a minority religion whose followers are scattered throughout the country, has distinguished itself and continues to do so through its important contributions to French society. But this positive adaptation to the modern world has not kept Protestantism from experiencing a relative decline in support, which does not seem to have affected some Protestant Churches as much: paradoxically, those that are more 'conservative' (the evangelical Churches) are growing. As in the past, Protestantism today is informed by a tension that is part of its nature: between, on the one hand, a liberal tendency that advocates freedom of judgment and minimizes the importance of dogmatic pronouncements, and on the other, a fundamentalist outlook that considers the Christian faith as representative of staunch beliefs and positions that require restrictions on the behavior of individuals and groups.

Although a minority in number, Protestantism in France is not a minority as the term is commonly understood in social terms: there is a disproportionately large number of qualified professionals, including teachers and professors, among Protestants, whereas there are fewer workers and employees than among the population at large (despite the existence of a working-class Protestantism in some areas, especially in the East of the country). The evangelical Churches (the Pentecostals in particular) generally recruit more members from working-class backgrounds than the Lutheran and Reformed Churches do. Beyond these social characteristics, Protestantism takes a paradoxical and challenging position in French nation and society. This religious minority is especially active in four fields: social work, ecumenism, sexual ethics and political culture.

*Social work*

Its charities, including institutions such as the *Asiles John Bost* (founded in Dordogne in 1848 by the pastor John Bost, son of Ami Bost, one of the 'apostles' of the Protestant Awakening in Europe) and the *Sonnenhof* (created in 1876 at Bischwiller in Alsace), both of which care for handicapped children, as well as its youth movements (federations at the high school and university levels; the Christian Unions of Young Boys and Girls; the Unionist Boy Scouts and Girl Scouts) have helped train many important figures in society and in the Church such as Michel Rocard, Prime Minister from 1988 to 1991. Members of the *Jeunes Femmes* movement played a decisive role in the creation of family planning in France. In 1997, a Protestant theologian, Catherine Trautmann, a member of the Socialist Party, became Minister of Culture and Communication and was also the Government's spokesperson. Earlier, as mayor of Strasbourg (elected in 1989 and re-elected in 1995), she had been the first woman in France elected mayor of a city with a population greater than 100,000. In 2008, senator Gérard Larcher, a Protestant member of the UMP (President Nicolas Sarkozy's party) was elected President of the Senate (who is empowered to take over temporarily as head of state if the President of the Republic dies or resigns). The *Cimade* (*Comité Inter Mouvements Auprès des Evacués*), an organization founded by Protestants at the start of World War II to assist refugees fleeing the regions of France near Germany, is now one of the most important organizations assisting the immigrant populations in France; it also participates in development projects in emerging countries. Services such as *S.O.S. Amitiés* (created in 1960 as a crisis hotline) became secular after having first been founded as Protestant organizations.

In addition to the many newspapers and magazines with a principally Protestant readership, weeklies such as *Réforme* (Paris) and *Le Messager* (Strasbourg) make sure that Protestant voices are heard in the greater sphere of French public opinion, as do programs such as *Présence Protestante*. Many magazines – including *Autres Temps* (Paris), *Foi et Vie* (Paris), *Etudes Théologiques et Religieuses* (Montpellier), *Revue d'Histoire et de Philosophie Religieuses* (Strasbourg) – give voice to Protestant thinkers in the intellectual world, alongside Protestant publishing companies (such as Labor et Fides, Editions Olivétan, and Excelsis). The Faculties of Protestant Theology in Paris, Montpellier and Strasbourg also contribute to the intellectual and religious influence of French Protestantism. In addition to these three faculties, there is also the Free Faculty of Reformed Theology in Aix-en-Provence, representing orthodox Calvinism, and the Free Faculty of Evangelical Theology in Vaux-sur-Seine.

*Ecumenism*

The Protestant churches participate in the *Council of Christian Churches in France*, which was created on December 17, 1987. It is comprised of representatives of the Catholic Church, the Protestant Federation of France, the Inter-Episcopal Committee of Orthodox Bishops and the Armenian Apostolic Church. Its purpose is to spur thinking and, when needed, to instigate joint initiatives in three areas: service, public expressions of faith, and the visibility of Christianity in society. The intransigence of the Catholic hierarchy, both on ethical matters and the issue of women priests, complicates relations between Catholics and Protestants without, however, undermining the commitment of French Protestantism to ecumenical dialogue. But the enthusiasm for this dialogue that characterized the 1960s and 1970s has been replaced by a more tempered ecumenism that puts greater emphasis on 'unity in diversity' than on an active search for unity. It is once again fashionable to be different. As a result, various movements reasserting Protestant uniqueness have appeared. These movements have grown in strength following certain initiatives of the Catholic hierarchy itself. For example the Jubilee in 2000, which was set in motion by the papal bull of November 29, 1998 in order to celebrate 2000 years of Christianity, was given a rather cool reception by Protestants, in France and elsewhere. In particular, the granting of a plenary indulgence on the occasion of this Jubilee especially irritated Protestants. The beatification in 2000 of Pope Pius IX, the father of the dogmas of papal infallibility and the Immaculate Conception of the Virgin Mary, as well as those included in the Syllabus of Errors of 1864 did not help improve relations. The same was true of the *Dominus Iesus* declaration, which stated that the Roman Catholic Church was the only 'true Church of Jesus Christ'. This declaration appeared to be incompatible with 'the spirit of Augsburg' that characterized the signing of the Lutheran-Catholic Declaration of 1998 on the doctrine of justification. According to the 1995 poll among those 'close to Protestantism', the young are less interested in ecumenism and identify more with Protestantism than their elders. They take ecumenism for granted, but they also see it as something compatible with asserting their own religious identities.

Given the number of marriages between Protestant individuals and those of other faiths, and the inclusion within its membership of a substantial number of people raised as Catholics, French Protestantism represents a minority with a certain power of attraction. French Protestants have had difficulties: only a minority of protestant parents succeed in passing on the Christian faith to their children; the percentage of followers who financially support their church has decreased slightly; and young people no longer participate as actively as before. Demographically speaking, this indicates the growth in a kind of neo-Protestantism that gives a different perspective to the ethnic Protestantism traditionally seen in France. These supporters of Protestantism, who are not of Protestant background, do not have the same relationship to the religion as born Protestants. As a result, they have a clear role in helping Protestant thinking move forward.

*Sexual ethics*

By defending an ethical stance of responsibility that insists on education and the individual's freedom of choice, Lutheran and Reformed Protestantism discovered they were in tune with the modern world. As believers in 'responsible motherhood', for example, Protestants are strongly in favor of modern methods of contraception, and they have been pioneers in the development of birth control in many countries. They are more divided on the issue of abortion, but a number of Protestant Churches do accept the controlled termination of pregnancy under certain conditions. However, this position, like the wide acceptance demonstrated toward homosexuality, stirs up heated opposition from some 'orthodox' Reformed Protestants and evangelicals who consider these liberal attitudes as contrary to the Bible. The issues around sexual ethics (contraception, abortion, and homosexuality) have often brought out differences of opinion not only between Catholics and Protestants, but also between Protestants themselves, especially between Lutheran/Reformed Protestants and evangelicals.

But some recent debates have redrawn the lines between each group. This was true of the debate in 1998-1999 on the *Pacs* (*Pacte civil de solidarité*), a form of civil union that gave some recognition to unmarried couples. The F.P.F. did not fully support the *Pacs*: it saw in this proposal "a demand for 'public recognition' of homosexual conjugality", which in its opinion meant that all forms of conjugality would be lumped together indiscriminately. The F.P.F. did not like the idea that the public recognition of homosexual conjugality could break the link between conjugality and parenting. Actually, the wide range of Protestant attitudes means that Protestants waver between a position that more or less accepts the institutionalization of gay couples (the endorsement of long-term relationships and everything that encourages them) and a position that refuses any blurring of the lines between various forms of conjugality. But Protestant groups clearly agree that the *Pacs* must not give gay couples the legal basis to adopt children or the right to have children by artificial insemination. In the past, Protestants have agreed that conjugality must not be subject to the necessity of parenting (recognizing the right of divorce and endorsing the legality of contraception), but they now wonder about the opposite situation: can the bond of parenting, which is not a contract, be entirely subject to the bond between two free and equal people living as a couple?

The F.P.F., like the Catholic bishops, did not officially participate in the demonstration in Paris on Sunday, January 31, 1999, which was organized by the 'Générations anti-Pacs' collective. But the *Associations Familiales Protestantes* group did participate, as did various Reformed and Evangelical Protestants. If this demonstration, where Protestants marched alongside Catholics, Jews and Muslims, in itself indicates significant changes in Protestant attitudes, this is precisely due to the criticisms and questions that the F.P.F. presented during subsequent discussions with the other religions about the *Pacs*. Although French Protestant thinking has in the past kept up to date with modern views on issues such as divorce, contraception and the relaxing of moral standards, they have now entered a more critical stage in their history, faced with changes in society that are tending to question the traditional institution of the family, comprised of a heterosexual couple with children.

In their opinion, these changes are weakening the symbolic order of society, and in particular the institution of parenting: in other words, as an F.P.F. document puts it, institutionality itself. Faced with such fundamental challenges, it is not surprising to see Catholic and Protestant positions converging on this issue, as well as greater agreement between Lutheran/Reformed Protestants and evangelicals. While modern norms of sexual ethics divided Protestants and Catholics and even split Protestants themselves into opposing camps, the sexual ethics of *ultramodernity* undeniably bring them closer together.

The new position adopted by Protestants refuses moral and cultural liberalism. Does this indicate the beginning of a movement of Protestants away from the left, seen as too permissive in the area of morals? We find a strong confirmation of this hypothesis in the substantial difference of opinion between Protestants and French people in general on the subject of homosexuality. A large majority of Protestants (63%) think that 'homosexuality is an acceptable form of sexual expression', but this is a much smaller percentage than for French people in general (77%). Here, we can see the importance that the evangelical point of view has assumed in the world of French Protestantism, as evangelical Protestants are less liberal than many Reformed or Lutheran Protestants on this issue and on many others (but more conservative tendencies also exist in the Reformed and Lutheran Churches). For example, in the 2005-2006 *La Croix-Réforme*/CSA survey, those people 'close to Protestantism' of an evangelical nature distinguished themselves from Lutheran/Reformed Protestants in taking a much firmer stance against homosexuality: only 31% of them felt that 'homosexual couples should be able to obtain recognition from the Church' (vs. 53% of Reformed Protestants and 50% of Lutherans). However, this CSA survey also demonstrated that left-leaning evangelical Protestants do exist.

*Political culture*

In France, Protestants are ardent supporters of secularity, particularly in schools. For example, a 1995 poll of those people 'close to Protestantism' revealed that 71% of them were very attached to the idea of secularity, a larger percentage than among French people as a whole (50%). Those French who identify themselves as being 'close to Protestantism' have more reservations than the French in general when it comes to so-called parallel beliefs: 52% do not believe in astrology at all, whereas this is true for only 37% of all French people; 71% do not believe in spells or witchcraft at all, compared with 57% for the total population.

Finally, they are more likely than the French as a whole to consider certain acts as morally wrong, such as tax evasion, speeding, or shoplifting. The fact that most Protestant Churches today allow women to become ministers also helps foster the image of Protestantism as a religion in touch with the present. Protestants remain very involved in social issues and are particularly concerned about ecological problems.

In recent years, the voting tendencies of Protestants came into line with the French as a whole. If this came up in discussion, it was typically to point out that the traditional affinity Protestants had for left-wing parties a historical association that prevailed until the postwar period was becoming less and less apparent and was even starting to disappear. But according to an IFOP poll carried out in 2007 before the presidential election that led to the victory of Nicolas Sarkozy, the political leanings of Protestants seem to have undergone a new transformation. Once again, their voting habits distinguish them from the rest of the French population, but now because they tend to support more right-wing parties. As a result, their political orientation approaches that of French Catholics, whereas in the past there was a noticeable distinction between Catholic and Protestant voting patterns. Nicolas Sarkozy's positions on work (one of his slogans was 'work more to earn more'), effort, taxation, and gay parenting have probably resonated with Protestants. The work ethic and the importance placed on personal effort are fundamental to Protestants, as are family values and applying oneself in school. Protestants are doing more than joining in with the return toward traditional values work, family, education, country that is becoming a generalized tendency of French public opinion. They are doing so with such intensity that they are approaching the political positions of French Catholics, who are much more right-wing than French people as a whole. This political ecumenism should be taken into consideration, as it is probably the sign of a new dividing line in politics, associated with questions of morals and civilization, particularly in the areas of family and sexual ethics.

The 2007 IFOP survey confirms these essential shifts. It first indicates that the traditional left-right division of the political spectrum is now overdetermined by questions that put issues of an anthropological nature on the political agenda (What distinguishes humans from other living beings? What constitutes gender difference? On what grounds should the relationship between an adult and a child be established?). This means that voters who are sensitive to the religious dimension of such questions make their electoral choices on the basis of these issues.

We have seen this phenomenon at work in the United States in 2004 when George W. Bush was re-elected president, defeating the Democrat John Kerry. In France, although good taste dictates that people should demonize economic neoliberalism, they tend on the contrary to venerate a hyperliberalism of morals. Fewer Protestants (59%) than French in general (67%) would like to see 'the state give a freer hand to businesses', thus demonstrating that they are aware of the dangers economic hyperliberalism poses to the social structure. However, they are wary of current trends toward a liberalization of moral values; we see this particularly when the institution of the family, defined as a heterosexual couple with children, is brought into question. Moral matters are behind the movement of Protestants to the right of the political spectrum. But they do not share the fears of many on the right regarding a supposed lack of security: whereas 41% of all French polled say that they don't feel safe anywhere, only 34% of Protestants agree with this statement.

Left- and right-leaning French Protestants differ greatly on many social issues, for example on how they feel about immigration. Whereas the total group of those surveyed in the 1995 poll are split on the issue (each possible answer was endorsed by 47% of the group), there is a substantial difference of opinion between the Protestants on each side of the political spectrum.

| | Total of those surveyed | Close to Protestantism | |
|---|---|---|---|
| | | Left-leaning | Right-leaning |
| French identity must be preserved by limiting the number of immigrants | 47% | 32% | 68% |
| France has traditionally been a country where we welcome immigrants | 47% | 66% | 25% |

In addition, as we have noted, French Protestants have today entered a critical stage, faced with changes in society that tend to question the family as an institution as well as the value of work. In our view, the ecumenical tendency of both Protestants and Catholics to move further to the right is the sign of a profound desire for the moral regeneration of individuals and society, a desire that is also found among Protestants whose political views tend more to the left.

## Future of Protestantism in France

Like other religious groups, the Protestant minority in France is faced with the transformations that are currently affecting religions and society. Christian Churches have been particularly affected by the new situation that these transformations have created.

The contemporary situation of religion, in France as in other European countries, is characterized more by the loss of social power on the part of religious institutions than by the disappearance of religious sentiment: the 'crisis of creeds' is answered by a multitude of individuals saying 'I believe', while creating their own personal religion. An institutional deregulation of religious phenomena seems to be taking place, with the development of a kind of 'do-it-yourself' movement involving religious matters. This means a more sustained level of individual initiative (with the dismantling of religious systems centered more on the community) and also a certain loss of religious culture (the words and images traditionally used to express the Christian faith are no longer understood and are sometimes subject to unexpected reinterpretations: for example the Resurrection is reinterpreted by some people in terms of reincarnation). The modern religious world is shifting, in the forms it takes in society and in language. A situation such as this favors the development of a competitive market in salvation, where small independent entrepreneurs come to try their luck (new religious movements and cults). Religion finds itself vulnerable to consumer choice, as people decide to follow the messenger or the group that responds best to their aspirations. This situation benefits religious populism and charismatic figures: when the person takes precedence over his or her function, when institutions have to some extent lost credibility, direct personal contact becomes the most important factor. A few heroes of the world of religion allow people to identify religiously with them without necessarily obliging these followers to maintain stable ties with a religious organization.

These transformations do not mean that Churches no longer benefit from a certain level of recognition as institutions playing their role in society. Public authorities still ask them their opinion on various matters (particularly ethical issues), and individuals uninterested in church activities (services in particular) may still feel that churches need to exist. The construction of churches in new neighborhoods is requested as much by non-religious people as by religious people, sometimes even more so, and many people still deal with the matter of death through churches: funerals, memorial services and so on. But between this respect for churches and the ill-defined reconfiguration of religion mentioned earlier, the issue of the socio-cultural foundations of religion must be addressed: the basis of its support in the society and the density of its ties to culture, which must be visible and recognizable enough to be handed down from one generation to the next. Are we confronted today with a kind of instant religion that manifests itself in quick flashes, lending itself to a sort of religious channel surfing? If so, the great challenge then is to stabilize the socio-cultural context and address the issue of handing down traditions. When a religion is very much in the minority, as with Protestantism in France, these challenges become even more apparent. But there are also challenges that are specific to Protestantism.

Some people have even seen a 'Protestantization of France'. Has France become Protestant? Far from it. But these commentators intend to underline the fact that France, despite being a country with a Catholic majority, has adopted Protestant values of individualism and freedom of judgment. To the extent that Protestantism has represented individualism the 'disenchantment of the world' (*Entzauberung der Welt*) as Max Weber put it and declericalization, and to the extent that it has insisted upon personal freedom and individual responsibility, it has actually made positive contributions to the advancement of the modern world. In France in particular, it contributed to the process of secularizing the state and public institutions: its minority status only made its role in this area that much more remarkable. But although Protestantism has been in tune with the process of modernization and has helped the secularization movement, does it still have a place in a fundamentally secularized and pluralist society? French Protestantism today is confronted with problems of visibility and identity. Its visibility problem comes from its over-adaptation to modern society, and its identity problem comes both from its willingness to be open to the rest of society and from its ecumenical overtures toward the Catholic Church. As religious individualism has also increased among Catholics, dissent from Church teachings has correspondingly grown stronger: there is thus a kind of Protestantization of religious sentiment within Catholicism itself. These changes and Protestantism's commitment to ecumenical dialogue mean that the question of Protestant difference and its relevance still remains.

As an active minority comfortable with secular society and open to ecumenism, French Protestantism today finds itself in question. In a society undergoing secularization, Protestantism's secularizing virtues were appreciated. But now that the process is more or less complete, the situation is different. Now that established religion is no longer seen as a major part of the power structure and people have freed themselves from the authority of priests and ministers, some, more interested in 'religious religion' than the secular use of religious forms (crosses as fashion statements and the like), would like to see Protestantism regain its spirituality. Furthermore, given the blurring of identities, there is a hope that French Protestantism will assert its identity more clearly, which would conflict with its strong commitment to ecumenism. In this context, it is easier to understand the development of a more militant form of Protestantism with a stronger identity, as seen in different Churches and evangelical movements. In France as in other countries, this form of Protestantism that insists on personal conversion (being 'born again'), and on public expressions of faith, enters into competition with Lutheran and Reformed Protestantism. It is not the growing presence of Protestantism in the social life itself which have changed the national identity of France, but the growing cultural and religious diversity of the population in general. On the other hand, the change is more marked in the French protestant world: a French Protestantism less systematically identified with the Reformed and Lutheran Churches and more perceived through a great diversity (from the Lutheran-Reformed Churches to evangelical and Pentecostal Churches and, among the last, to the African, Asian and West Indian Churches). This evolution has led to a more ambivalent and complicated image of Protestantism in the French society: a religious minority in which there are not only liberal-progressive wings generously open to the today cultural evolution, but also more orthodox-conservative wings conservative refusing clearly the individualistic and hedonist trend of these evolution.

## Further reading

Bréchon, P. & Tchernia, J.-F. (eds.). (2009). *La France et ses valeurs.* Paris: Armand Colin.

Dargent, C. (2005). *Les protestants en France aujourd'hui.* Paris: Privat.

Fath, S. (2005). *Le protestantisme évangélique en France 1800-2005*. Geneva: Labor et Fides.
Willaime, J.-P. & Cusenier, D. (1998). *Protestantisme.* Paris/Besançon: Cerf/CRDP de Franche-Comté.
Willaime, J.-P. (2002). Les apports de la sociologie à l'étude du protestantisme français contemporain. *Bulletin de la Société d'Histoire du Protestantisme Français, 148*(4), 1011-1033.
Willaime, J.-P. (2002) Entre éthique de responsabilité et éthique de conviction. L'éthique sexuelle en débat dans le protestantisme français des années 1970-2000. In J. Maître & G. Michelat (eds.), *Religion et sexualité* (pp. 59-72). Paris: L'Harmattan.
Willaime, J-P. (2005). *Sociologie du Protestantisme*. Paris: PUF.

# Islam in the Netherlands

## A nation despite religious communities?

Thijl Sunier

### Introduction

As is the case with most Western European countries, the Netherlands has witnessed the emergence of Islam as a result of large-scale immigration. In 2008 there were around 900,000 people with an Islamic background, comprising about 6 percent of the total population. Turkish Muslims constitute the largest group (372,000), followed by Moroccans (335,000), Surinamese (45,000), Pakistanis (50,000), Iraqis (45,000), Afghans (38,000), and Iranians (30,000). The remaining population with an Islamic background comes from Somalia and some other African countries (Centraal Bureau voor de Statistiek [CBS], 2008). There are also a relatively small number of Muslims from Indonesia - about 10,000 according to estimations - and a small proportion from other East-Asian countries. There are currently an estimated 12,000 converts to Islam in the Netherlands.

Unlike in France or the United Kingdom, only a small proportion of the Muslim population comes from former colonies. Before the Second World War there were already small Muslim communities in the Netherlands from the former Dutch colonies of Indonesia and Surinam. The impact of the Dutch colonial past on its academic heritage is impressive. The University of Leiden is renowned for its archives of old Islamic texts, and it was the principal place where administrators for the colonies were trained. The Netherlands once dominated the most populous Muslim area in the world (Indonesia, former 'Dutch Indies'). Yet it was not until the large-scale post-war immigration that Islam took root in the public imagination. Postcolonial conditions play no part in the debate on Islam in the Netherlands and the colonial past is largely ignored. Migratory conditions, however, are very central parameters of Dutch policies on Islam. For a long time hardly anyone realized that with this influx of so-called guest-workers, a 'new' religion had also entered the Netherlands. Initially, Islamic practices remained hidden behind the walls of the boarding houses where the single male migrants lived. On special occasions such as Ramadan, Muslims were sometimes able to make use of factory halls or churches to perform their religious duties. It was only on these occasions that the wider society became aware of their presence (Sunier, 1996).

Until the end of the 1970s the government and society considered the presence of Muslims to be a temporary phenomenon. Islam had come to the Netherlands as 'cultural baggage' by labor migrants who would soon return to their home countries. The few who would remain, it was thought, would gradually assimilate into Dutch society, which itself was in the middle of a process of secularization and modernization. Thirty years later the idea of Islam as a residue from another type of society that would soon fade away has partly been falsified. In the early 1970s there were only a few provisional places of worship. A decade later there were about a hundred permanent 'mosques' and currently there are a little over 450 mosques: permanent, public places (though not always visible from the outside) of worship run by an Islamic organization. But also in other respects, Islam has become more visible to the outside world. Muslim families settled in the old quarters of the main cities, where they opened their own shops and teahouses. Children went to school and in 1988 the first Islamic primary school was opened. Currently there are more than thirty Islamic schools. In many spheres of life, special arrangements have been made to enable Muslims to live according to Islamic prescriptions. It is clear that in the past 35 years, Islam has gained a foothold in Dutch society. Muslims have managed to create a religio-cultural infrastructure and to give Islam a public face. This has been referred to as the institutionalization of Islam (Landman, 1992; Rath et al., 1996; Sunier, 1996). This chapter addresses these conditions and describes how the Netherlands have dealt with this new religious and ethnic diversity over the past decades. It also attempts to show how the debate on the position of Muslims has influenced discourses on Dutch citizenship.

The Netherlands, like other Western European countries, grant religious freedom to all religious denominations. The opportunities for Muslims to set up a religious infrastructure are generally conditioned by constitutional principles of freedom of religious worship and the separation of church and state. It would, however, be a gross misunderstanding to consider the integration process as unilinear and unconditional based on these principals alone. The parameters of the process are generally dependent on a complex of factors and outcomes are unpredictable. The process is characterized by a complex set of long-term historical, and mid and short-term political factors. These not only structure the way in which institutionalization takes place, but it also shapes the discourses of identity, nationhood and citizenship and the ongoing debates about the place of Islam in society. I will look at three dimensions. Firstly the general conceptions of citizenship, nationhood and modes of inclusion and exclusion. Secondly aspects of relations between religion and state. And thirdly, the position of migrants. Although minority policies and religious issues are formally separate spheres, there is a clear relation between the two.

## Religion and the Dutch state

Apart from the general principles of freedom of religion and the separation of church and state, there are three main constitutive factors that have influenced the place of Islam in Dutch society. The first is the constitutional principle of religious equality. The Dutch Constitution of 1983 stipulates that all religious denominations are equally valid. Although this principle of equality actually dates back to the liberal Constitution of 1848, the idea was reinforced and reformulated in 1983 by severing all the financial and other ties between churches and state. An important aspect of the equality principle is that the Dutch system, unlike that in Belgium or Germany, does not apply the principle of religious recognition and registration. Thus there are no religious denominations in the Netherlands that have formally more privileges than others. Equality means equal treatment in similar situations. Although there actually is still much inequality between established denominations like the Reformed and Catholic churches and 'new' religions like Islam and Hinduism, this principle of equality has indeed offered Islamic leaders a legal and political leverage to demand equal treatment and, in some cases, extra provisions in order to be able to catch up with established denominations.

The second factor relates to the era in which Dutch society was organized along confessional lines, from the 1920s till the 1960s. Dutch society consisted of so-called 'pillars', corporate religious communities or blocs that dominated the political landscape. The Dutch pillar system is one of the more complicated aspects of Dutch political history. During those forty years, there were two confessional pillars, a Catholic one and a Protestant one. In addition to that there was a Socialist movement and a so-called Liberal sphere. The two confessional pillars comprised more than 50% of the Dutch population and ran through all social classes.

They had their own political parties, trade unions, schools, universities, media and all kinds of other associations. The churches were at the heart of these pillars. The Socialist movement, though not a pillar in the literal sense, was actually organized as one, although it had its political base mainly in the working class. These three blocks were organized from top to bottom and exerted a great influence on their rank-and-file. The ruling elite of the Liberal sphere was economically the strongest fraction in society, but from a social-organizational point of view it was the weakest. It was mostly composed of people who were not affiliated with one of the three other blocks and it adhered to the principles of the liberal Constitution of 1848.

An important characteristic of the system was the strong emphasis on sovereignty of the pillars. The two confessional pillars especially demanded no state interference whatsoever in matters that were related to the daily life of the rank-and-file. Although these kinds of politico-ideological divisions were not unique for Europe, the way in which the system almost completely shaped and determined political relations during that period is. It was also the political (to some critics rigid) stability that was so characteristic. This generally accepted stability rendered the system its seemingly 'natural' character. Despite the dividedness there was a strong feeling of belonging to one nation, which was not yet the case in the 19th century. The blocks were principally considered equal and balanced to one another. Social conflicts were pacified and neutralized by closely cooperating ruling elites at the top of the four blocks. Due to the rigidity of the system political developments were extremely slow in the Netherlands between the 1920s and 1960s. The system continued to shape political relations for a considerable period of time even after the Second World War.

Towards the 1960s the system lost its function and in most sections of civil society a breakdown of the pillar structure took place. These politico-ideological blocks not only determined to a large extent the political relations in the Netherlands; they also fragmented the Dutch population. Precisely for this last reason, there have always been political factions that were rigorously against the pillar system since it would divide rather than bind society. We may conclude that the process of de-pillarization took on a specific ideological shape in Dutch politics as a process of 're-uniting the Dutch people' and of rebuilding the Dutch nation on new principles.

Although the societal forces that sustained the pillarization process have today almost completely been replaced by the centralizing mechanisms of the modern welfare state, the juridical remnants of the system do still play a role in some crucial areas. The most important is the Dutch school system. The Dutch educational system is still largely pillarized in that so-called confessional (*bijzondere)* schools not only have exactly the same state (tax) funded material resources as public (*openbare*) schools (equality principle), but also because the relative autonomy of the various school types is still a crucial element in educational politics. These principles of equality with respect to education were officially effectuated by the constitutional changes of 1917, the so-called *pacification laws.* Public education is organized and administered by the state. Confessional schools have their own administrative boards. Originally most of them were of Christian (Catholic or Protestant) origin. In addition to that there were some Jewish schools and 'Free schools' (anthroposophical). Their number grew after the Second World War. Since the post-war immigration, Islamic and Hindu schools were added to the list. Although there is today a steady increase in number of public schools, still the majority of pupils at primary schools are enrolled in confessional education. Important, however, is that the basic curriculum is similar and obligatory in all school types. This curriculum is the state's responsibility. The difference between public and particular schools is mainly a matter of educational style, extra-curricular activities and additional religious education (Sunier, 2004).

Other areas that are organized on the basis of juridical provisions originating in the pillar system are the broadcasting system and pastoral welfare work in hospitals and prisons. Although secularization took place even at many confessional schools, the system is still one of the most delicate issues in Dutch politics. Muslims can relatively easily make use of these provisions and since the end of the 1980s a little over thirty state-financed Islamic primary schools and one secondary school have been founded. Even more important than these formal and legal remnants of the era of pillarization is the fact that pillarization can be found at the heart of a typical Dutch discourse or even myth about tolerance and mutual respect between the religio-cultural segments of society. It also largely explains the relatively easy way with which minorities are defined along religious lines and the idea that members of religious denominations constitutes religious communities that are organized as a pillar in the Dutch (historical) sense.

The third factor concerns Dutch integration policies. Muslims are generally considered migrants and as such they are subject to the specific requirements and aims of the Dutch integration policies that have been set up and developed since the early 1980s. The parameters of these policies, including the important shifts that have taken place since the early 1980s, indicate the trajectories towards a domestication of Islam. Islam has rendered the status of 'immigrant religion', its features and characteristics are part and parcel of the cultural background of immigrants, people from outside the Dutch nation-state. Policies are designed to make these people members of Dutch society, not as members of a religious denomination but as individual immigrants (Rath et al., 1996). It is important to note that Dutch integration policies do not deal with religious diversity as such. For example it is strictly speaking incorrect to consider Islamic schools as part of these integration policies. In practice, however, the integration debate is highly relevant for the development of the school issue. These fields are discursively and politically connected.

Key terms of the Dutch integration policies are permanent residence and the participation of migrants in Dutch society together with a (limited) recognition of cultural diversity. Thus, according to the Constitutional principle of freedom of religion, Muslims have the right to set up their own religious infrastructure. They can also make use of the juridical provisions that enable them to found their own schools, provided this should in no way hamper the integration process of migrants. The shifting and ever-changing interplay between these constitutive factors over the past decades have rendered meaning to the typical Dutch notion of citizenship. Thus in the early 1980s there was a strong tendency to treat religious accommodation set up by Muslims as an intermediary between immigrants and the host society. This resulted in a heated debate about the extent to which the Dutch government should support institutionalization of Islam as a tool of the integration policies. The paradox that emerged here was that material support may have unintended consequences of stabilizing religious accommodation while the integration policies aimed at assimilation of immigrants.

The structural conditions sketched above should in no way be treated as determinative. As I have argued in the introduction to this volume, in order to understand how political culture is reproduced and articulated, we should consider neither religious affiliation and religious traditions, nor the structural and ideological dimensions of the nation-state as independent variables. Political culture is the outcome of a continuous process of negotiation and struggle in which structural, normative and ideological conditions play a crucial role. The outcome, however, is principally unpredictable because we can in no way know all the relevant factors that account for cultural dynamics. In hindsight the Rushdie Affair in the early 1990s, and the 9/11 backlash more recently were unintended events with unintended consequences.

In the following section I will present an historical account of the Dutch policies on Islam roughly over the past three decades. I will show how periods of relative silence (see Aminzade, 2001) alternate with periods of highly mediatized contention.

## Migrants, Muslims, ... citizens?

Until the end of the 1970s, the cultural and religious background of migrants did not play any significant role in debates about their position in society. Migrants were defined in terms of ethnic origin, but this had no political consequences. Officially the Netherlands did not yet see itself as an immigration country. Migrants were primarily seen as members of a temporary labor force who would return to their countries of origin. Policies were based on this idea of temporariness. The creation of religious facilities was therefore seen to be something that should be left solely to private initiative. No special policies were needed; it was believed to be a self-regulating process (Sunier, 1996).

Towards the end of the 1970s important developments took place. The number of immigrants increased considerably, mainly due to family reunions. These families settled in the old quarters of the main town centers. Although for the vast majority of Muslims returning to their country of origin was still their intention, the actual return was postponed. Many migrants could not afford to return home. As a consequence, the need for religious facilities increased, especially the need for qualified religious personnel (Landman, 1992). At the same time organizational structures improved and activities increased. Many mosque organizations developed into real cultural centers for migrants. There were teahouses, shops and other facilities. Also in this period for the first time attempts were made by various local Muslim associations to work together, to improve communication and to coordinate activities. The number of religious organizations grew steadily. It was, however, a development that hardly caught the attention of the wider Dutch society.

*1980s*

Towards the beginning of the 1980s a turning point was reached. For the first time the government acknowledged that the idea of temporariness was unrealistic. The majority of the migrants were set to stay here permanently. In 1983 the government issued a report in which the outline of a new policy was formulated. It was at this point that the concept of 'integration with the preservation of identity' (*integratie met behoud van identiteit*) was introduced (Ministerie van Binnenlandse Zaken [BiZa], 1983, pp. 38-42; Werkgroep-Waardenburg, 1983). Migrants were granted basic rights to live according to their own cultural background; whilst at the same time they were expected to integrate into society. This became the typical Dutch trajectory to full citizenship. 'Integration' was narrowed down 'participation' in the central sectors of society: labor, housing and education (Engbersen & Gabriëls, 1995). Along with this concept of integration the term *achterstand* (best translated as deprivation) made its way into the discourse. A lack of integration was equated with *achterstand* and vice versa. Equality, a central concept in integration policies in the early 1980s, should be understood here as equal opportunities (of migrants and indigenous population). It did not refer to an idea of cultural equality. The misconception of these terms and the policy implications are the reason why the Netherlands of the 1980s is still seen as a country with multicultural policies (Sunier, 2010).

During the 1980s the government adopted a lenient attitude towards cultural diversity. In the first place there was the general notion of culture and religion as basic properties of human beings. Thus the relevance of cultural background for a persons' wellbeing should be acknowledged (BiZa, 1983). On the pathway to full citizenship the relevance of culture and religion for the people concerned was recognized as a psychological outlet. Immigrants should have time to adapt to the new circumstances and this could best be accomplished in 'their own circles'. Organizations of migrants would therefore function as a bridge between the individual migrant and society in order to ensure a smooth integration of migrants into society. As such they gained more significance in the integration process. They were politically and ideologically incorporated into the government's policies (Rath & Sunier, 1993). Islamic organizations were considered important organizations of migrants, and their activities were judged on their functions in the process of integration. It was expected that once integration has succeeded, these organizations would gradually disappear. Organizations could now apply for subsidies to develop activities for their rank-and-file, provided these activities sustained the integration process. This is fundamentally different from granting basic cultural rights as 'would-be' pillars. I have described this discursive process as the 'migrantization' of Islamic organizations (Sunier, 1996). One of the consequences was that the number of organizations grew significantly in the course of the 1980s.

Some critics of Dutch integration policies of the 1980s have contended that the principle of 'integration with the preservation of identity', so typical for Dutch minority policies originated in the pillarization history, a sort of multiculturalism *avant-la-lettre*. This is not true. Instead of characterizing these policies as multiculturalist, as has been done in debates during the course of the 1980s and 1990s, they should be traced back to the American assimilationist perspective as developed in sociology in the 1950s and 1960s (Sunier, 2010). This perspective has been introduced and elaborated for the Dutch situation by Van Amersfoort (1974). His view on integration became the basis for Dutch minority policies in the 1980s. An important aspect of this new policy was that a relation was constructed between integration on the one hand and cultural background on the other. 'Guest workers' were renamed as 'ethnic minorities', 'cultural minorities', or 'ethnic groups'. In other words a shift in the definition of the situation took place. Migrants were moved from an economic category to a cultural one. Cultural background became relevant in integration policies. This is one of the most complicated aspects of Dutch integration and citizenship policics.

Whatever their origin, the policies adopted in the 1980s were on the whole certainly not unfavorable for Islamic organizations (*as migrant organizations).* At the same time, however, there was also a concern about the attitude of Muslims and their organizations towards the principles and priorities of the integration program developed by the government. The new policies of integration took shape at a time when dramatic events, such as the revolution in Iran and the assassination of the Egyptian president Sadat, were taking place in the Islamic world. These events caused a tremendous increase in the number of publications about Islam and its adherents. Suddenly migrants from countries like Turkey and Morocco were 'discovered' as Muslims. A new cultural category emerged: 'Muslim migrants'. For convenience's sake, people with completely different backgrounds were lumped together under the heading of 'Muslim culture'. Since it was mostly

Muslims facing problems of deprivation with respect to housing, labor and education, 'Muslim culture' rendered specific meaning.

Islam increasingly became the explanatory factor, not only for specific (collective) behavior of Muslims, but also for all kinds of societal problems they faced. This 'islamization of the discourse', often led to a narrower outlook: 'when one wants to know what goes on in the head of a Muslims then one should study Islam'. All other possible explanations were in fact reduced to 'the' Islam (Rath & Sunier, 1994, p. 57). Although this line of thinking was not to be found explicitly in official documents, it was part of the public considerations about Islam expressed in newspapers and magazines, in statements by individual politicians in Parliament and on television. Besides that, there was a growing interest in Islam and its adherents among welfare workers and other people working with and for Muslims in various situations.

As a result, a specific image of Islam made its way into public discourse. It is an image based on the idea that Muslims are the least integrated migrants. Just as the Netherlands are saying goodbye to religion as a binding force in society, a new religious group appears and asks for provisions that had almost disappeared. A religious group that is known for its anti-modern character, it was assumed. According to this view, Muslims are seen as passive, fatalist people who are turned inwardly and face difficulties catching up with the pace of modern society, and easily fall back on their faith. One of the main objections to the foundation of Islamic schools, for example, is that they cause undesirable isolation of young children. Islam enforces rules upon them that inhibit them from taking part in society.

The origin of this image can be related to the so-called 'rural bias'. A majority of the first generation Muslim migrants have a rural background. They stand for the archetype 'Muslim'. Rural habits and Islamic prescriptions are constructed into an amalgam that represents the religion as a whole. Despite the negative undertone in this type of discourse, boundaries between 'them' and 'us' are not conceived to be impermeable. There is a certain inclusiveness and compassionate undertone in this image. Muslims are not fundamentally excluded as a separate category; it is their faith that enforces rules upon them. But these problems can be overcome through systematic socialization. The boundary may be temporary, provided certain conditions are fulfilled (Rath & Sunier, 1997, p. 59).

As a result of the political and ideological developments that took place in the 1980s, a new type of Islamic leadership emerged. These leaders had lived in the Netherlands for a relatively long time; they knew society quite well and had acted as an intermediary between Muslim migrants and Dutch society. They were entrepreneurs rather than 'ideologists' and were oriented towards mobilizing as many resources as possible. They successfully made use of their contact with Dutch policymakers and institutions. They emphasized that Islamic organizations must be considered as the main forms of 'self-organization' among migrants. These leaders increasingly took part in discussions on the position of migrants and as opinion leaders they gained influence. They represented the Muslim populations and articulated what needs existed among Muslims. They also articulated what it means to be a Muslim in a non-Islamic society. By stressing the 'foreign' character of Islam, as something that is part of the cultural heritage of a specific group of migrants, they were able to convince policymakers that certain facilities were required (Sunier, 1996).

*1990s*

Towards the end of the 1980s there was a turning point, due to several new developments. With respect to minority policies, the lenient attitude towards the preservation of cultural identity and the prominent role that had been given to migrant organizations came under pressure. In an advisory report, the influential Scientific Council for Government Policy (WRR) warned the government of the continuing weak socio-economic position of minorities (WRR, 1989). Unemployment figures among migrants remained relatively high and educational results remained below the expected levels. In short: integration was considered bound to fail unless the government laid more emphasis on the struggle against poverty and deprivation, if necessary at the cost of cultural programs. Notions of the collective integration of certain minority groups were increasingly replaced by an emphasis on an individual trajectory to full-scale integration into the so-called 'hard' sectors of society, such as education and labor market. More than before, participation in the central institutions of society became the key goal of integration policies. General programs of combating poverty and deprivation gradually replaced specific programs for specific groups.

In addition to that, the image of Islam in the country changed considerably. The 'migrantization of Muslims', the discursive strategy that aimed at inclusion and that characterized most of the policies until the mid 1990s, turned much more into a discourse of exclusion in which Islam was seen as a foreign element. It was also the time when the term ‘allochtonous’ (and ‘autochtonous’ for that matter) made its way into public debate. Geschiere (2009) argues that the dichotomy between allochtonous/autochthonous has spread rapidly in the last decades, not only in Europe but also in Africa and Asia. It is an explicit purifying discourse that excludes all those who do not belong to an imagined autochthonous community. The term has spread at such a pace in the Netherlands that it can now be considered the most powerful trope in minority relations. As a direct consequence of the Rushdie affair, a new type of image emerged. This image links Muslims in the Netherlands to the violence in the Middle East. Muslims are conceived as a fifth column that may be a threat to society. This has resulted in an ongoing debate about growing fundamentalism among migrants, worries about connections between Muslims here and fundamentalist groups in the Middle East and worries about the strong orientation of Muslims towards their country of origin.

The main difference with the first image is that boundaries are conceived to be impermeable. Muslims constitute a different ‘brand’. They will never become part of Dutch citizenry unless they abjure their religion completely. They do not fit into the Dutch nation, since it is not the preservation of culture that they aim at, but transnational political activism. One of the leaders of the Dutch liberal conservative party, Bolkestein, considered Islam to be the main threat to European liberal civilization. Muslims should be monitored carefully, he said in 1991 (Bolkestein, 1991).

*2000s*

It will come as no surprise, then, that the events of September 11$^{th}$, 2001 reinforced this image and made it the dominant one in almost all countries in Western Europe. September 11$^{th}$ not only caused a relative strengthening of this image, but also a shift in argumentation against Islamic institutions such as schools and mosques. Even Christian Democrats, traditionally strong defenders of freedom of education, began to doubt whether this freedom should be granted to Islamic schools. These schools should at least have to prove that they did not teach ‘against the central values of Dutch society’. In the last few years the number of incidents related to Islam and to the presence of Muslims has increased tremendously. Imams are being scrutinized, and every public statement is weighed as a possible ‘danger’ for society. Most importantly, however, is the growing consensus among Dutch politicians over the need to control the institutionalization process and to emphasize assimilation into Dutch society. An increasing number of people have serious doubts about the possibility of Muslims becoming fully-fledged citizens while at the same time retain to their religious convictions. Islam has increasingly become associated with undesirable influences from abroad. Islam became foreignized. This is a fundamental breach with the Dutch pillarized political culture of the 20th century. Nation-building today is determined by global anxieties about Islamic threats and by a rapidly diminishing trust in the effects of integration policies.

## Conclusions

From the late 1980s onwards there were two main, contrasting positions in the public debate over cultural diversity, multiculturalism and Islam in the Netherlands. These positions were not just political ideals, rather they relate to one or more aspects of the actual Dutch political culture. The first position was slightly revised version of the liberal view on individual rights. It envisioned society as being made up of individual citizens who have an equal relation to the state, and integration is an individual trajectory into the central institutions of society. Equality is a principle of individual citizens. Cultural diversity is subservient to this principle and members of religious or ethnic groups cannot claim specific collective rights based on cultural peculiarities with respect to their position in society, since this would jeopardize equality. At this point the approach resembles the French republican model. This does not mean, however, that cultural peculiarities are to be discarded completely (see also Van Rooden and Massignon in this volume). The state should acknowledge that culture has an important impact on an individuals' wellbeing, so there must be room for cultural and religious expression. At the same time all individuals have a moral responsibility towards the nation as a whole. They should be prepared to enter into a social contract with the state and with society and to subscribe to the liberal principles central to the nation-state.

If we compare the French model in which citizenry is defined as a territorial community and where civic incorporation is based on the *jus soli* principle, and also that of Germany where the understanding of nationhood and citizenship is based on descent (Brubaker, 1992, pp. 81-82), then the Dutch version of citizenship can be described as 'contained pluralism', or 'plural equality'. The model is in some respects similar to the American 'nation of nationalities'. The Netherlands is today acknowledged to be an immigration country with migrants from different ethnic backgrounds, which in terms of the integration trajectory it follows the French assimilationist logic. Through a coherent program of economic and educational measures structural inequality between migrants and native Dutch should be removed. Once this is accomplished everybody can take part in society on an equal basis without denying ethnic or religious specifics. As far as material equality is concerned, it is assumed that ethnic differences will become irrelevant and may eventually fade away completely.

The other more communitarian view hinges on the idea that the history of pillarization in the Netherlands offers a relevant framework for the development of a model that grants certain collective rights to religious groups. According to this view it is unrealistic to deny the fact that the Netherlands is now a multicultural society with all its associated political implications. Although the collective emancipation of religious denominations at the beginning of the 20th century led to the fragmentation of society into confessional blocks, at the same time it contributed to the building up of the Dutch unified nation. In this respect the Dutch system resembles that of Great Britain in that it envisions society as made up of groups and communities, notably ethnic or religious groups. The pillars were the principal integrative devices in the Dutch nation-state. In a modern society that is made up of new and old ethnic or religious groups integration into society evolves in a similar way. Supporters of this view question the fear of liberals that an emphasis on ethnic and religious autonomy jeopardizes the integrity and unity of the nation. Recognition of religious diversity and the granting of collective rights to religious denominations will not infringe on the goals of the governmental policies of civic integration (*inburgering),* it is argued (Klop, 1994). Integration policies thus play a crucial role in the Dutch multicultural debate. One cannot understand the different positions without taking these policies into account.

Recent developments have caused a remarkable shift in these two political positions. Liberal constituencies in the Netherlands are now divided into two groups. A diminishing proportion prefers to the old encompassing liberal ideals of religious freedom and religious equality. They envision a society not of culturally distinct groups, but of equal and distinct individuals. But there are an increasing number of liberal politicians who consider liberal ideals to be a system of political values that excludes rather than includes Muslims. To a certain extent they envision liberalism as an exclusivist ideological position that competes with other worldviews. Society is no longer a diversified public realm, but a battleground that requires winners and losers (see also Schinkel, 2007).

The Christian Democrats, traditional supporters of the multicultural position and still one of the bigger political constituencies in the country, have more or less abandoned the idea of value relativism that was dominant during the heydays of pillarization, preferring instead a political program that places religions and cultures in a hierarchical order. These shifts have resulted in a growing consensus among both liberals and communitarians on the necessity of cultural assimilation. Concepts of citizenship in the Netherlands today, therefore, converge on the same assimilationist model.

## References


Aminzade, R. (2001). *Silence and voice in the study of contentious politics.* Cambridge: Cambridge University Press.

Bolkestein, F. (1991). *Address to the liberal international conference at Luzern*. Den Haag: VVD.

Brubaker, R. (1992). *Citizenship and nationhood in France and Germany.* Cambridge: Harvard University Press.

CBS (2008). *Jaarrapport integratie 2008*. Den Haag: CBS.

Engbersen, G. & Gabriëls, R. (eds.) (1995). *Sferen van integratie: Naar een gedifferentieerd allochtonenbeleid.* Amsterdam: Boom.

Geschiere, P. (2009). *Perils of belonging: Autochthony, citizenship and exclusion in Africa and Europe.* Chicago: Chicago University Press.

Klop, C.J. (1999). Religie of etniciteit als bindmiddel? *Migrantenstudies, 15*(4), 246-254.

Knippenberg, H. (1999). The ethnicity of national integration: Religion, education and politics in the Netherlands. *The Netherlands' Journal of Social Science, 35*(1), 37-53.

Landman, N. (1992). *Van mat tot minaret: De institutionalisering van de Islam in Nederland.* Amsterdam: VU Uitgeverij.

Ministerie van Binnenlandse Zaken (1983). *Minderhedennota.* Den Haag: BiZa.

Rath, J. & Sunier, T. (1994). Angst voor de Islam in Nederland? In W. Bot, M. van der Linden & R. Went (eds.), *Kritiek: Jaarboek voor socialistische discussie en analyse, 93-94,* (pp. 53-63). Utrecht:

Stichting Toestanden.
Rath, J., Penninx, R., Groenendijk, K. & Meyer, A. (1996). *Nederland en zijn Islam: Een ontzuilende samenleving reageert op het ontstaan van een geloofsgemeenschap.* Amsterdam: Het Spinhuis.
Schinkel, W. (2007). *Denken in een tijd van sociale hypochondrie: Aanzet tot een theorie voorbij de maatschappij.* Kampen: Klement.
Stuurman, S. (1983). *Verzuiling, kapitalisme en patriarchaat: Aspecten van de ontwikkeling van de moderne staat in Nederland.* Nijmegen: SUN.
Sunier, T. (1996). *Islam in beweging: Turkse jongeren en islamitische organisaties.* Amsterdam: Het Spinhuis.
Sunier, T. (2004). Naar een nieuwe schoolstrijd? *Bijdragen en Mededelingen betreffende de Geschiedenis der Nederlanden, 119*(4), 552-576.
Sunier, T. (2010). Assimilation by conviction or coercion? Integration policies in the Netherlands. In A. Silj (ed.), *European multiculturalism revisited.* London: Zed Books.
Van Amersfoort, H. (1974). *Immigratie en minderheidsvorming: Een analyse van de Nederlandse situatie 1945-1973.* Alphen aan den Rijn: Samson.
Werkgroep-Waardenburg (1983). *Religieuze voorzieningen voor etnische minderheden in Nederland: Rapport tevens beleidsadvies van de niet-ambtelijke werkgroep ad hoc.* Rijswijk: Ministerie van WVC.
Wetenschappelijke Raad voor het Regeringsbeleid. (1979). *Allochtonenbeleid.* Den Haag: WRR.

# The governance of Islam in France

## Church-state traditions and colonial legacies

Marcel Maussen

### Introduction

Over the past decades, Muslim communities in Western Europe have set up a range of institutions serving for their religious, social, cultural and educational needs. The resulting patterns of institutionalization of Islam vary; in part because of diverging national regimes of governance of cultural and religious pluralism (see Maussen, 2007). In an insightful analysis of French church-state institutions and more contemporary forms of treatment of Muslims, the American anthropologist John Bowen draws distinctions between a Gallican tradition of state control over religions, a Concordatarian tradition of official recognition and collaboration with 'organized religion' (*le culte*) and various interpretations of secularism that co-exist underneath the signifier *laïcité* (Bowen, 2007, p. 1006). If one conceives of national regimes of governance as 'historical products', it seems plausible to compare present day policies of accommodation of Islam to the particular ways the French state has dealt with religious newcomers in the past. A case in point is the accommodation of the claims for recognition that were articulated by Jewish minorities at various moments in French history (Cohen, 2009; Jansen, 2006; Safran, 2003).

Our understanding of contemporary forms of state accommodation of Muslim religious practices would benefit from more historically sensitive studies. Yet, in my view there is a risk if the historical approach mainly consists of attempts to juxtapose and compare, on the one hand, more recent policies of accommodation of Muslim populations and, on the other hand, responses to earlier waves of (European) immigration and to the ways the French dealt with religious pluralism in the $19^{th}$ century. Such a comparison privileges the idea that there exists a distinctive French model of governance of religious pluralism and national integration which is shaping responses to immigration and religious newcomers, irrespective of *who* these immigrants are and irrespective of *what religion* we are talking about. Thereby the relevance of French colonial history for the governance of Islam and Muslims is being obscured. France has been involved with the governance of Muslim populations and Islam in ways it has not been with the governance of other religions. In addition, it has been demonstrated convincingly that policies of migration control and accommodation of non-European 'colonial subjects' differed sharply from strategies of incorporation developed vis-à-vis other, white European, immigrants. A recent study, for example, shows how in the 1930s, French governments subjected Algerian Muslim immigrants to "much greater disciplinary controls than any foreigners" (Rosenberg, 2006, p. 206). Instead of writing a general history of French immigration policies and seeking to explain these in light of French traditions of citizenship and nationhood – that is along the line of the seminal studies by Noiriel (1988), Brubaker (1992) and Weil (2004) - several recent studies focus especially on the specific characteristics of policies of immigration and accommodation of colonial and post-colonial populations, such as the Algerians (Blanchard et al. (eds.), 2005; MacMaster, 1997; Shepard, 2006; Stora, 1992).

In this chapter I reconstruct French governance of Islam over a period of about 150 years, beginning with French colonial policies in Algeria and West Africa and reaching unto the first decade of the 21st century. Public policies vis-à-vis Muslim religious needs and Islamic institutions should be understood against the background of cultural ideas, political concerns and policy goals and these varied according to broader regimes of incorporation (Maussen, 2009). My aim is to demonstrate the ways distinctive governing strategies were developed and institutionalized, and how these were then reproduced, as well as contested and changed, over time. I distinguish three broader regimes of incorporation: a colonial regime, a guest workers regime and a citizenship regime. I conclude that colonial governing approaches and especially the will to control Muslim institutions have influenced French post-war policies of accommodation of Islam to a far stronger degree than is usually acknowledged.

## French colonial policy and Islam

With the intensification and extension of French colonial rule in North and West Africa in the late 19th and early 20th century, colonial administrations increasingly began to face issues related to the governance of Islam. In Algeria the Convention of Bourmont, which had marked the surrender of Algeria's Dey in 1830, had formally assured that the French would guarantee the right to Islamic practice. Nonetheless, during the first years of the French conquests many mosques and Muslim cemeteries were destroyed and later the French expropriated the possessions and land of the religious foundations (*habous*), thereby depriving the Algerians of the means to finance the costs of their religion. Officers of the *Bureaux Arabes*, regional administrative bureaus which informed and advised the colonial administrators, were given complete authority over all matters touching on Islam. Policies of selective cooperation and state regulation that were characteristic of the Concordatarian tradition of religious politics were mixed with strategies to co-opt indigenous leaders who were supportive of French colonial rule. French governance thereby led to conflicts between the confraternities, the 'official clergy' and the 'independent' *Ulama* (Bozzo, 2006, p. 207.).

Initially, the French were ambiguous about the role Islam would play in the process of expanding colonial rule and in relation with the 'civilizing mission'. The French believed, for example, that the Berbers valued the Islamic faith far less than the 'Arabs', which led them to think that the Berbers could be more easily assimilated into French culture than the 'fanatically religious' Arabs (Lorcin, 1995). In West Africa the appreciation of Islam and indigenous culture was different. The French had created alliances with Islamic scholars and they had used Arabic as the lingua franca during the expansion of colonial rule. They thought that the introduction of Islam constituted a clear form of cultural progress in West Africa when compared to the existing 'animistic religions'. Islam would introduce intellectual culture, societal organization, a commercial spirit and education, and these amounted to a higher form of civilization (Cruise- O'Brien, 1967, p. 305).

French administrations progressively sought to extend their control over Islam in the African colonies, fearing the growing influence of reformist Islamic movements and the ways Islam served as a constant inspiration of opposition to colonial rule. In 1902, the fiercely anti-clerical French minister, Émile Combes, proposed to make Islam an officially recognized religion in the African colonies. The leaders of the religious brotherhoods would be placed under French supervision and they would become a sort of official clergy. This would help the French administrators in their installment of moral reforms. Combes' proposition wasn't enacted, but the French would develop a clear set of guidelines to govern Islam in both Algeria and West Africa. Importantly, the religious policies that concerned Islam and Muslim populations would increasingly diverge from the governing strategies developed in France following the 1905 Law on the Separation of Churches and the State.

Because Algeria was an integral part of France and given that secularism and the separation of church and state were among those high values of modernity championed by the French civilizing mission, it seemed reasonable to expect that the new secularist legislation would now also be implemented in Algeria. In 1907, however, a special decree was issued which laid down a modified application of the principle of *laïcité* in Algeria. It enabled the French colonial authorities to continue to remunerate the 400 official '*agents du culte musulman*' and sponsor the mosques and Madrasas. Since the 1920s the official imams were selected on the basis of an exam and a personal dossier, which should serve to determine whether the candidate had a sufficient degree of 'loyalty towards France' and whether he had some influence upon his fellow believers (Achi, 2005, p. 169). After the Second World War a new law was issued in Algeria in 1947 which was to give more guarantees for the independence of Islam vis-à-vis the state. A special commission on the regulation of Islam in Algeria was also established. This commission suggested creating a single council representing Algerian Islam and to let this council be in charge of the places of worship and the management and financing of Muslim religious practice (*le culte*). Islamic scholars (*Ulama*), who tried to found independent mosques as an alternative to the 'official' French mosques, protested against that proposition. Also, the French Council of State argued that the installment of an official Algerian Muslim council opposed the principle of the separation of church and state. However, fearing that the complete separation might possibly jeopardize French colonial rule in Algeria, the Algerian subdivision of the French Ministry of the Interior issued a new text in 1950 which discussed the implications of the principle of separation of church and state for the North African colony. This text suggested that the principle of *laïcité* could not be fully applied to Islam in Algeria. The reason for this was that there were "some resistances" amongst the native population, who "remained faithful to the concept of a theocratic State, which controls both earthly and spiritual matters, which is the traditional conception in Islamic countries" (cited in Achi, 2004, p. 86 [my translation, M.M.]). The French thus legitimized their strategy of financially supporting and fostering a co-opted, loyal Islam in Algeria until the country became independent in 1962.

In West Africa, the French administrators developed a very different policy (see Cruise-O'Brien, 1967; Harrison, 1988). As stated, the French initially believed Islam to constitute a form of cultural progress. But at the end of the nineteenth century, fear took root that the influence of pan-Islamic ideas in Western Africa would eventually come to undermine French rule. Colonial administrators worried that by making Arabic the lingua franca in Western Africa they had unintentionally contributed to the spreading of Islam. Also, at the end of the nineteenth century, the appreciation for indigenous and animistic religions gained traction. The French now concluded that in West Africa a specific form of Islam had developed: African Islam (*l'islam noir*). In the African 'variant', Islam was mingled with local cultural traditions where through Islam was relieved of 'fanaticism', which, according to the French, was characteristic of Arab Islam. Therefore it would be necessary for the colonial administrators to shield 'African Islam' as much as possible from further Arab and North African influences. In Western Africa, Islam could be developed further on the basis of 'French ideas' and with the help of colonial rule it could become a modern religion (Harrison, 1988, p. 97). French support for a moderate, loyalist Islam and the shielding of syncretized forms was complemented with a policy of surveillance of other branches of Islam. Maintaining French rule in place was valued over the principle of separation of church and state and over the freedom of religion for Muslims.

In view of understanding the relevance of colonial strategies of governance for the post-colonial period it is crucial to realize how these overseas Islam policies became of increasing relevance for French foreign policy and for experiences in France itself. France's ambition to be recognized as a Great Muslim Power (*La France, Grande Puissance musulmane*) led to the wish to further develop strategic alliances with selected religious leaders in the colonies, and with religious and political rulers in the Levant, North Africa and the Middle East. Around the First World War the Ottoman-German alliance rallied Muslims to join their side and fight against the French and English unbelievers with the aim of ousting them from the Middle East and Northern Africa. The French military authorities reacted to this propaganda by portraying France as a 'friend of Islam' (*La France, amie de l'islam*). At the same time, thousands of young men from the colonies were mobilized as soldiers and workers. Efforts were made to provide for the religious needs of Muslims. In Marseille in 1916, a project was developed to copy a complete Algerian mountain village which could house colonial laborers and where a mosque was also to be built (Maussen, 2009, pp. 69-72). Imams could also visit the military camps, in the military hospital in Neuilly a prayer room was created, in the colonial garden of Nogent-sur-Marne a wooden mosque was built, and at the Muslim hospital in Bobigny an Islamic cemetery was opened in 1937 (Le Pautremat, 2003). One of the most important events in this context was the construction of the Paris Mosque between 1922 and 1926.

The idea to build a mosque in the French capital originated in 1846 in discussions of the *Société Orientale*, but the project gained traction in 1916 when the French Inter-ministerial Commission for Muslim affairs (*La Commission Interministérielle des Affaires Musulmanes*, CIAM), that was responsible for French war propaganda and contacts with North Africa and the Middle East, learned about the construction of the mosque (MacMaster, 2002, p. 72; Le Pautremat, 2003). The building of the mosque in the centre of Paris would be perceived as an important gesture and this sign of 'respect for Islam' would amount to a show of support for the co-opted Muslim leaders. After the war it was proposed that the mosque be a monument for Muslim soldiers who perished in the French armies. The Paris Mosque was eventually built in the fifth arrondissement near to the *Jardin des Plantes*, in a typical North African style. The building included a prayer area, baths, and a Moorish café. The costs of the construction were – despite the separation of church and state – paid with a gift from the French state and the city council of Paris, and with various gifts from Muslim countries. One of the co-opted North African Muslim leaders – Si Kaddour Ben Ghabrit – was chosen as chairman of the mosque, a function he would hold until his death in 1954. The mosque would accommodate travelling notables from friendly Muslim states and Muslim elites who visited Paris and it would also to cater to the Parisian bourgeoisie who would be able to visit the mosque to drink a cup of mint tea and enjoy the exotic ambiance. The North African immigrants living in the Paris region, including 60,000 Algerian migrant workers, were discouraged from using the mosque. Colonial workers were expected to make use of other prayer halls, such as the places in the hostels located in the suburbs. Not surprisingly therefore, the most outspoken protests against the construction of the Paris Mosque came from those who cared primarily about the plight of the colonial workers in Paris and who challenged the colonial system itself. The leader of the nationalist movement *Étoile Nord-Africaine* (ENA), Messali Hadj, organized a protest against the opening of the mosque in 1926 attended by some 200 migrant workers. A communiqué proclaimed that the 'so-claimed mosque' was being inaugurated in the presence of those

North African leaders who "still have red hands from the blood of our Muslim brothers" (cited in Bayoumi, 2000, p. 287).

The creation of the Paris Mosque and the co-optation of Abdelkader Ben Ghabrit were also important in forging additional institutional linkages between the governance of Islam in Algeria and policies of accommodation in France. These linkages would also extend into the post-colonial period, when in the French government and the leadership of the Paris Mosque would continue to join together in order to exercise influence on the development of Islam in France.

## Islam in post-colonial times and the recruitment of foreign workers

Already in the 1930s guest worker programs had existed in France in which the government and companies collaborated to recruit foreign laborers, both in the colonies and in other European countries (Cross, 1983). From the 1950s onwards, foreign workers were being recruited anew to provide the growing French industry with much needed cheap labor. Traditionally, European foreign workers had the possibility to settle in France and to gradually be absorbed into French society. The North Africans, on the other hand, were not particularly welcome and they were perceived as more culturally different because of their skin color but also because of their Muslim religion. French colonial officials and military officers in North Africa repeatedly warned their colleagues in France to keep a close eye on the workers because there was a great risk of intemperance when they "escaped from the Muslim environ ment" (in Le Pautremat, 2003, p. 283 [my translation, M.M.]). French authorities were also particularly apprehensive of the idea of French women marrying Muslim men (Le Pautremat, p. 287). North Africans were kept segregated from mainstream French society and they were 'repatriated' when there was no more work for them. French scientists and policy advisors in the 1930s thought that it would be impossible to assimilate certain races in French society, especially "Asian and African elements" (in Weil, 2004, p. 38).

These differences between the situation of European and colonial guest workers were also being institutionalized as special instances were created to accommodate North Africans. Institutions such as the *Service de Surveillance, Protection, et Assistance des Indigènes Nord-Africains* (SAINA) and the *Service de l'Organisation des Travailleurs Coloniaux* (SOTC) were designed to combine surveillance, control and assistance for North Africans (Rosenberg, 2006). After the free circulation of Algerians to and from France was ended because of the Algerian War in 1956, French authorities wanted to be able to control the Algerian population in order to prevent the shantytowns and squatter camps becoming bastions of the National Liberation Front (FLN). A semi-public property management organization was set up that was responsible for worker housing and should finance, build and equip foyers (hostels or homes) for Algerian migrant workers. It was called *Société Nationale de Construction de Logements pour les Travailleurs Algériens* (SONACOTRAL). Only after 1962 other foreign workers could also be housed in its hostels and its name changed to SONACOTRA. This system of foyers for foreign workers was one of several institutional arrangements that were already in place in the colonial period and that continued to function after Algeria and other African colonies gained independence and new generations of immigrants from these countries came to France. In addition, the handling of immigration and the accommodation of North Africans in France since the 1960s was in a significant part carried out by people who had been formerly employed in the administration and services of colonial rule. In 1975, 144 out of 151 hostel directors working for the SONACOTRA company were army veterans, and 141 of them had worked in Algeria.

The kind of reception and institutional arrangements North African and West African immigrants would meet in France until the late 1970s was by and large a continuation of what had existed in the colonial period. With regard to the treatment of Muslims two aspects merit to be highlighted. First, in contrast to the experiences of other immigrant groups and despite the fact that Muslim immigration dated back to the early 20$^{th}$ century, Muslim religious institutions, such as the mosques, could never develop into mature associations that could become gravitation centers for an ethnic community infrastructure. In a city such as Marseille where Algerian communities lived for many decades, Muslims were compelled to worship in impermanent prayer spaces until the mid 1980s. Initiatives to construct a real mosque, which dated back to the 1930s and 1940s, had all failed (Maussen, 2009). The situation of other immigrant communities developed very differently in that respect. Many immigrants set up an ethnic community infrastructure that was organized around their religious institutions. In Marseille the image of self-supporting ethnic communities and a flourishing religious life among immigrants was frequently represented as illustrative of the successful integration of Italians, Corsicans, Greeks and Spaniards. Nothing comparable existed for Muslim immigrants.

Second, the different perception of North African immigrants also mattered for the ways French authorities sought to accommodate the religious needs of Muslims in the context of guest worker programs. In 1976 a draft immigration policy was issued that spoke of the risk of North African immigrants in France becoming 'uprooted'. This was said to result from social and cultural isolation. Many immigrants were living in cities while they originally had come from rural areas and they were also cut off from the spiritual ties that in "Islamic countries play an essential role in the collective and individual equilibrium". Seen in this light: "Religious practice and being able to have access to a place of worship would help the Maghrebians to recreate in France one of the important moments of their daily life" (cited in Kepel, 1991, p. 141 [my translation, M.M.]). The Under-Secretary of State for Migrant Workers at the time, Paul Dijoud, planned to provide for the religious needs of Muslims by creating a Muslim television broadcast on Sunday mornings, creating possibilities for Muslim spiritual care in hospitals and prisons, encouraging municipalities to create Muslim cemeteries and encouraging company directors to facilitate respect for Muslim religious rules with respect to dietary requirements and prayer. In 1976 he sent out a directive which laid down a program in favor of cultural action for the immigrant population. This program included among its headings 'Support for the establishment of houses of worship'. In the neighborhoods where many Muslims lived places of worship were to be put at the disposal of the believers because "traditionally, for the Muslims, the cultural life cannot be separated from the religious duties" (cited in Kepel, p. 143 [my translation, M.M.]). Because Under-Secretary of State Dijoud disappeared from the scene for political reasons, even before the text explaining the New Immigration Policy was published in 1977, the implementation of these ideas was gravely compromised. The idea of developing a nationwide effort to help create prayer houses as part of a *'promotion culturelle'* was not really executed.

By this time, however, immigrant workers were better able to protest against the hostility, violence and discrimination they were confronted with in France. In 1975, a nation-wide protest movement had developed in the foyers when tenants refused to pay the rent, and demanded the improvement of their housing, the right to receive visitors and the lowering of the rent (Ginésy-Galano, 1984). Another central demand of the residents was to have facilities for Islamic practice, such as prayer rooms and ritually prepared food. The protest movements in the hostels were followed in 1982 by protests by North African migrant workers in French industries. Strikes were held in the automobile industry of Renault and Citroën. The strikers eventually succeeded in getting their employers to comply with their demands for prayer rooms, ritually prepared food and special breaks to allow them to accomplish the daily prayers (Kepel, 1991, pp. 145-159). The administrators of the foyers came to think that the possibility of having adequate prayer rooms would be perceived as a significant symbolical gesture by the Muslim residents. It would therefore help to keep social peace at relatively low costs (Kepel, p. 126). Between 1976 and 1986 80% of all foyers in France were equipped with prayer rooms. This operation was subsidized by the public-private property management organizations that were responsible for workers housing.

The fact that French authorities and employers were involved in helping to improve the housing conditions of some of these prayer rooms, though not in a very forthcoming way, does not really match with existing ideas about the importance of *laïcité* for the governance of religion in France. However, these forms of support were not primarily seen in terms of public authorities financing religion or of public officials responding to Muslim claims for recognition. They were motivated both by the idea that helping immigrants to retain their religion and culture might facilitate their return to the countries of origin, and by the idea that helping Muslims to create and equip elementary religious spaces was not fundamentally different from helping to provide for other socio-cultural needs.

## Citizenship and Islam

Colonial and guest workers policies had institutionalized and legitimized unequal treatment, segregation and hierarchy between Muslim immigrants and the host society. When Muslims came to be seen as permanent members of French society and acquired French citizenship, these representations and practices had to be redefined. In this final section I discuss policies of accommodation of Muslim religious practices since the early 1980s.

*The 1980s: The marginal position of Islam and the Republican model*

In the early 1980s the overall orientation in French public policies vis-à-vis the social problems of migrant communities had been pragmatic and there had been some support for the idea that temporary migrants had a right to retain their cultural distinctiveness (*droit à la difference*). However, by the end of the decade these ideas were renounced in favor of more ideologically loaded policies of integration. Immigrants should emancipate and integrate as citizens and they should not create their own ethnic and religious institutions and organizations (Favell, 1998, pp. 46ff.). At the same time, partly because of the uprising of the Front National in the 1980s, it became clear that a great amount of resistance existed against immigration and the presence of Muslims.

Many migrants had moved with their families to affordable social housing which was erected in large quantities in French cities. Small mosques and prayer rooms were created on the ground floor or in basements or garages of the flats, which gave rise to the expression 'the Islam of the basements' (*l'islam des caves*). There wasn't much protest against the realization of these prayer rooms, also because they were part of largely self-contained urban forms where immigrant communities were concentrated. When Muslims wanted to create more permanent, larger or more prominent prayer houses they would often be confronted with lack of interest or outright hostility. When the mayor of Marseille, Gaston Defferre, was informed of plans to make a mosque in the city center more prominent and visible, he reportedly said to the chairman of the Mosque Committee: "Make a place ... but don't make it there... it is the entrance of the high way... I don't want the tourists who come to Marseille to see the Arabs leaving the mosque" (in Maussen, 2009, p. 54). The building of new mosques – in Évry and in Mantes-la-Jolie – was also accompanied by resistance and fierce protests (De Galembert, 2005). Muslim communities were still compelled to practice their religious freedoms in sheds and garages. Not many politicians were willing to go out on a limb with propositions to alter the unequal treatment of Muslims and the Front National received high electoral outcomes with slogans like "Chador, Mosque, Enough! ("*Tchador, Mosquée, Assez!*").

At the end of the 1980s, however, here and there ideas arose to also make room for Muslim communities. Islam became more visible in French society for a number of reasons. Academic studies were published that spoke of the existence of 'a new religious community' in France. Social scientists who took interest in Islam in France were mostly opposed to government embracing a form of multiculturalism and researchers stressed that it would be wise to help Islam to further institutionalize itself in France, play down the influence of foreign governments and international organizations, and encourage Muslims to orient themselves more within a French social context. The best ways to incorporate Islam was via the development of an 'Islam of France' (*un Islam de France*). There were three possible disruptive elements that could prohibit a gradual integration of Islam in French society. In the first place there was Islamic fundamentalism. The fear that Islamic fundamentalism might gain traction in France gained in popularity, especially because of the developments in Algeria, where a civil war erupted after the success of the Islamic Salvation Front (*Front Islamique de Salut*, FIS) at the elections for parliament in 1991 (Kepel, 1994, pp. 233ff.). In the second place, it would be dangerous when Muslims in France would become strongly divided along ethnic lines. The enduring existence of ethnic groups within French society meant Muslims hadn't been able to free themselves from the influence of their countries of origin, which would seriously impede their Republican citizenship. Muslims in France needed to be 'integrated' (*intégrés*) and this would also keep them from the dangers of 'fundamentalism' (*intégrisme*) (Kepel, 1991, p. 379). The third threat to the integration of Islam was the growing aversion of migrant youths to the French state as a result of existing forms of discrimination. The fact that France lagged behind other European countries with regard to opportunities for Islamic practice might allow extremist Muslim organizations to rally support with exactly these marginalized youngsters from the suburbs. This particular mixture of worries and expectations informed initiatives to develop strategies of governance of Islam in the late 1980s and early 1990s.

Different ideas about the ideal development of Islam in France came together around the notion that the bigger cities of France should allow for the building of 'Cathedral mosques' (*Mosquées Cathédrales*). These Grand Mosques could become the institutional seat of the leaders and representatives of the Muslim community in that particular city. The Cathedral Mosque could also become a symbol of recognition that could take away feelings of discrimination and it would illustrate the emergence of an 'Islam of France' (Maussen, 2009). In the fall of 1989, the mayors of France's two largest cities next to Paris – Marseille and Lyon – presented ideas to build such a central mosque. The mayor of Marseille, Robert Vigouroux, stated in *Profession Politique* of October 29:

> I want it to be an attractive building. In first instance for the city. But such a mosque should also be a symbol for the Muslims of Marseille. Somewhat like the Cathedral is for Christians. *Mosquée-hangars* might be necessary, but they are also unworthy. I don't want this mosque to be visited merely by Muslims, but also by other people, like the *Marseillais*, tourists, and foreign visitors. It should become something that triggers curiosity.

However, the mayor also formulated a number of preconditions for the project to be carried through. The mosque would only be built when there was a request of "the representatives of Islam in Marseille" and it should become an "instrument of integration" that would not come under the control of any foreign government. Soon it became clear that it was unlikely that Muslims would come up with a consensual project for a central mosque. Furthermore, public and political protest against the plans grew rapidly. Representatives of the Front National argued that the Muslim newcomers threatened the Christian identity of Marseille. Protesters had the wind of public opinion in their sails. The expulsion of two Muslim girls from a public school in Creil in early October 1989 led to the first so-called headscarves controversy and led to a wider debate on Islam, *laïcité*, integration, women's emancipation and fundamentalism.

Events in Marseille were illustrative for the ways these early attempts to accommodate Muslim demands for recognition often ran into trouble. Not only was there widespread hostility against North Africans and political opposition against the growing visibility of Islam, the various policy objectives often existed in tension with one another and conflicted with the demands of Muslims. Attempts to impose the idea that the 'public sphere' should be neutral and secular collided with demands by Muslim women to wear the headscarf, attempts to co-opt 'liberal' Muslim leaders in order to create an 'Islam of France' existed in tension with the principle of separation of church and state, and the blunt refusals by many municipal governments to accommodate basic religious needs of Muslims were fuelling to the idea that Republican discourse was a fraud because in reality immigrants were being discriminated against. One of the main challenges remained to find interlocutors with enough legitimacy to make sound agreements on issues that were now on the agenda.

## The 1990s: Islam of France and the privileged position of the Paris Mosque

A guiding idea for efforts to steer the development of Islam was that some sort of representative institution needed to be created that could speak on behalf of 'the French Muslims'. If there was one institution in France that desired such a role, it was of course the Paris Mosque. After the ownership of the Paris Mosque had been handed over to the Algerian government in 1982, the institute had tried to develop a network of mosque organizations all over France. The Paris Mosque also appointed imams that would, in part, be remunerated by the Algerian state. Since 1992 the institute was presided over by Dalil Boubakeur, who positioned himself as the unavoidable partner for French authorities. A constant theme in the self-positioning of the leaders of the Paris Mosque was that they alone were able to obstruct the spread of Islamic fundamentalism in France. With support of the Algerian government the Paris Mosque had, not unsuccessfully, tried to find political supporters, notably in the circles of the Right (Geisser & Zemouri, 2007). This strategy paid off when a new government of the Right acceded to power in 1993.

The new French government would seek to impose an organizational model upon Islam in France. In December 1994 a text for a 'Charter of the Muslim Religion' (*Charte du Culte musulman*) was written up which was co-signed by the new Minister of the Interior, Charles Pasqua. The charter would serve to create a new Representative Council of the Muslims in France that would function under the aegis of the Paris Mosque. The Paris Mosque also became the only institution officially qualified to monitor the production of ritually sacrificed meat and to levy a tax on it. Almost simultaneously, in September 1994, the Minister of Education Bayrou had issued a directive requiring school principals to ban all 'ostentatious' religious signs, especially headscarves, from schools (Bowen, 2006, p. 89). The actual effects of the strategy of privileging the Paris Mosque would be limited, also because a new government of the Right acceded to power in 1995. The new Minister of the Interior, Jean-Louis Debré, did not pursue the same strategy and, for example, the monopoly of the Paris Mosque on the certification of halal products was ended in 1995. It had become clear that the growing importance of other Islamic associations and federations, such as the *Union des organisations islamiques de France* (UOIF) and the *Fédération nationale des musulmans de France* (FNMF), could not be denied. One reason for their growing visibility in the institutional landscape was that these Muslim organizations counted many younger Muslims among their constituency.

At the end of the 1990s it became clear that Muslims in France still had great difficulties in making effective use of their religious free-exercise rights. In response to this situation the Minister of the Interior in the government of Lionel Jospin, Jean-Pierre Chevènement, initiated a Consultation in November 1999, in view of developing representative bodies and institutions that would allow Islam to "join the other religions at the table of the Republic". During this Consultation various issues would be discussed, including the need for an institute to train imams, the regulation of the market for 'religious products' and the creation of more and better mosques and Islamic cemeteries.

The lack of adequate Islamic religious facilities was also signaled by the French High Council on Integration Policy (*Haut Conseil à l'Intégration*, HCI) which published a report on 'Islam in the Republic' in 2000. Only eight genuine mosques with visible minarets existed in France, although the total Muslim population in France amounted to five million believers. Allowing for the building of Grand Mosques seemed a way of addressing this shortage of adequate prayers spaces while simultaneously responding to demands for recognition raised by younger generations. An editorial of *Le Monde* published on March 10, 2001 was entitled 'constructing mosques':

> Is it acceptable that Muslims, followers of the second religion in France, are still forced to practice their religion in too small and uncomfortable places for worship? That Muslims (...) are required to roll out their prayer rug on the pavements of our cities? (...) The incorporation of a 'Cathedral Mosque' in the urban landscape stimulates the integration of Muslims, many of whom have French nationality. Because, beyond the needs of the worshippers, the establishment of a Grand Mosque is first and foremost a symbol: it represents the integration and recognition of Islam.

Effectively, various French cities developed projects to realize new mosques. Among them were cities such as Strasbourg, Montpellier and Marseille (Maussen, 2009). Local struggles on the building of larger mosques took place against the background of a broader discussion on the future of Islam in France.

The societal context was now characterized by reactions to the terrorist attacks in the United States of 2001. At first it was believed that the attacks formed a justification to speed up the institutionalization and recognition of Islam. Some believed that the creation of adequate facilities and institutions for a 'moderate' Islam could prohibit feelings of resentment gaining traction amongst young Muslims in France. Others argued that many so-called well-integrated Muslims might be dangerous 'extremists in disguise' and 'integrated extremists' (*intégristes intégrés*). The growing importance of a new generation of assertive young Muslims who based their demands for recognition on a discourse of citizenship, equality and religious freedom could also constitute an opportunity to enter into a new phase in the governance of Islam in France.

## The 21st century: The French Council of the Muslim Religion and 'vicinity Islam'

The process of Consultation on Islam (1999-2003) included very concrete steps to create representative Muslim councils at different institutional levels (local, regional and national), but it also included a wider set of goals concerning the future of Islamic worship. If the state would become more directly involved in the creation of Muslim institutions this created opportunities for French authorities to insist that Muslim leaders declare their support for key constitutional principles such as secularism, equal treatment and religious freedom. These attempts entered a decisive phase when Nicolas Sarkozy became Minister of the Interior in May 2002. Sarkozy's approach to the creation of the French Council of the Muslim Religion was a combination of Gallican and Concordatarian strategies, and it earned him the name of the Napoleon of Islam in France (Bowen, 2006, p. 100). He sought to overcome the older strategy of almost exclusive cooperation with the Paris Mosque and insisted that a broad range of Muslim denominations and 'schools of thought' would participate. Nonetheless, Sarkozy tried to organize the formation of the future Muslim Council in such a way that 'moderate' voices would be represented. French officials were closed involved and orchestrated the process in such a way that the outcomes of the 'democratic elections' for the Muslim Councils would be acceptable, especially for the Paris Mosque and for the French authorities. When the Council was installed for the first time in 2003 Dalil Boubakeur became the president while representatives of the other major federations were appointed as vice-presidents.

The formation of the Muslim Council and the events of 9/11 were not the only factors resulting in an almost continuous public discussion on Islam in France in the early years of the 21st century. The widely mediatized hearings and deliberations in 2003 of the Commission of Reflection on the Application of *Laïcité* in the Republic, also known as the Stasi-commission, and the controversies on the headscarf also contributed a fair share. The parliamentary vote in February in favor of a law banning all conspicuous signs of religious affiliation from public schools seemingly meant further legal and political legitimacy for Republicanism and *laïcité*. However, one should not forget that the 2004 ban gave a boost to Republican values in a specific institutional and policy domain – the public schools – and with respect to a specific aspect of the presence of Islam, namely the display of religious identity by wearing the headscarf. This should not be equated *tout court* with French public policy responses to Islam in this period.

Actually, between 2004 and 2007 progress was being made in addressing practical concerns and providing for religious needs. Special national penitentiary chaplains were installed both for the military and for the penal system, who were to coordinate the activities of the official Muslim chaplains that were remunerated by the French state. There were new policy proposals to create training facilities for clergy, notably imams and chaplains, and the government intended to complement the religious curriculum of the training program with state-sponsored secular teaching. The construction of Muslim cemeteries was also an issue under consideration. These policies were informed by concerns about equity, effective religious freedom and cooperation. One of the policy domains in which a quite far-reaching change of direction occurred concerned the issue of mosque building. In the early years of the 21st century, a new perception of the smaller makeshift mosques had come to prevail. Many mosque associations and mosque users had enlarged, improved and renovated their prayer spaces. Often they had put a nicer new carpet in, painted and decorated the interior and made the place for the ritual ablution prettier, for example by paving it with North African tiles. A vocabulary gained in prominence to speak of these places without discarding them as inadequate. They were called 'neighborhood mosques', 'pavilion-like mosques' and 'discrete prayer houses'. As a correlate of the more positive reputation of the 'neighborhood mosques' there was also a vocabulary to speak of the organization of Islam at the city district and neighborhood level: the so-called 'vicinity Islam' (*islam de proximité*) or 'neighborhood Islam' (*islam de quartier*). Prominent scholars of Islam in France spoke of a 'normalised Islam' that was 'tailor made' (*sur mesure*) and of the forming of so-called 'Muslim parishes' (Frégosi et al., 2006, pp. 45ff.). The growing positive view of the neighborhood mosques came at the expense of the idea that it was necessary to build large and noticeable mosques. According to the critics, the true recognition of Islam in France required that Muslims be allowed to decide themselves on what kind of mosque buildings they deemed adequate and appropriate.

These new ways of perceiving mosque buildings and the development of 'vicinity Islam' greatly affected local policies which became more pragmatic in their orientation and sought to accommodate 'normal' religious needs. Municipalities became involved in making inventories of the needs and the situation of houses of worship and of being of help in the relocation and renovation of neighborhood mosques. An important policy goal become to see to it that the 'neighborhood mosque' was well incorporated and accepted and that, by consequence, 'vicinity Islam' could function as an integrated part of the daily life in the neighborhoods (Frégosi et al., 2006, p. 54). On October 26, 2006 the director of the Central Bureau of Religious Affairs, Didier Leschi, declared in an interview with the newspaper *La Croix* that the 'Islam of the basements' no longer existed. He confirmed the estimates made by the journalists of the total number of Islamic prayer houses in France going up from 1,555 in 2001 to more than 2,000 in 2006 and explained that at present France was in a phase of "accelerated catching up".

The national government also picked up on this new approach and tried to support municipal governments to facilitate the creation of cemeteries, facilities for ritual slaughtering and adequate houses of worship. In February 2005, the Ministry of the Interior issued a directive addressed to the prefects, calling upon them to remind municipal authorities to see to the respect of legal regulations and not to obstruct the building of places of worship for inappropriate reasons or on illegal grounds (Maurer, 2006, p. 44). In addition there were initiatives to further regulate the financing of mosques in France. On March 21, 2005, representatives of the UOIF and other major Muslim federations signed the statutes allowing for the creation of a Foundation to Finance Islam in France (*Fondation pour les oeuvres de l'islam de France*). The foundation, created under private law, was categorized as accomplishing a public interest (*d'utilité public*) meaning among other things that the

French state could directly interfere with its administration (Maurer, pp. 46-47). In the Fall of 2007 the foundation had become a reality. Significantly, the rector of the Paris Mosque, Dalil Boubakeur, was now also appointed as the president of this foundation.

A second idea under discussion was the possibility of revising the legal framework and modernizing the 1905 Law on Separation of Churches and the State. In October 2004, Nicolas Sarkozy had suggested that it should be possible to consider to "further develop" (*faire évoluer*) the 1905 law in order to allow for a direct financing of mosque building. Back in office as Minister of the Interior since May 2005, Sarkozy decided to create a *Commission de réflexion juridique sur les relations des cultes avec les pouvoirs publics*. That commission, presided over by the legal scholar Jean-Pierre Machelon, would advice on the need for and the possibilities of amendments to the 1905 law. The Machelon Commission published its report in September 2006 and suggested allowing for direct subsidies for the building of houses of worship for disadvantaged immigrant communities. Such a measure could be inscribed in the legal practice and tradition of the 20$^{th}$ century, so the commission argued, because the French state had always, in specific circumstances, been involved in stimulating the building, repairs and upkeep of religious buildings. Moreover, it would be a manifestation of the willingness of the Republic to show its concern for those social groups that were facing disadvantages, and would create more transparency in the financing of houses of worship (Machelon, 2006, pp. 26ff.).

This attempt of some influential legal scholars to give a new turn to the ongoing discussion on the meaning of church-state arrangements in France led to a storm of protest. Advocates of strict or militant secularism (*laïcité de combat*) stood up in public, political and academic debate to protest against what they saw as an attack on *laïcité*. Following the critical reception of the report, Nicolas Sarkozy, presidential candidate at the time, already announced that he did not intend to follow up on the recommendations and would not modify the text of the 1905 law. In October 2007, however, a new working group of legal advisers was installed to study the recommendations of the commission and come up with a proposal to the government. The outcome of this process was the publication by the Ministry of the Interior of a new directive in May 2009. This directive serves to clarify the legal regime and existing jurisprudence with regard to public financial support for the creation, restoration and upkeep of houses of worship.

These recent shifts in French policies towards Muslim religious needs show how different sets of governing strategies continue to exist within French church-state traditions. Whereas the regulation of religious symbols in the domains of the state and in public schools continues to be linked strongly to secularism, the ways the state is involved in the organization of Muslim representative bodies is greatly indebted to colonial and Concordatarian traditions. In allowing for direct and indirect support for the improvement of religious facilities, French authorities draw on yet another aspect of their church state traditions, which is also laid down in the first article of the 1905 Law that stipulates that the Republic "guarantees freedom of conscience and the free exercise or organized religions".

## Conclusion

Most of the literature on Islam in France has sought to explain public policy responses since the late 1980s in light of reified ideas about the French model of integration and its emphasis on Republicanism and *laïcité*. However, for most of the 20$^{th}$ century policies of accommodation of Muslim immigrant populations were being shaped by colonial and guest workers regimes. The historical development of the accommodation of Muslim populations created possibilities for patterns of governance to continue shaping public policies in subsequent periods. French colonial policies were extremely well institutionalized and the principle of secularism was consistently sidelined in the governance of Islam. Strategies of control and surveillance prevailed and the French tried to secure support for their rule over the North and West African colonies and protectorates by backing co-opted leaders who represented an official and loyalist Islam. When Muslim sojourned in France as soldiers, colonial workers and later as transient guest workers, French public authorities were willing to contribute - also financially – to the creation of minimum provisions for religious needs, such as ritually-prepared meals and prayer rooms. In the 1960s and 1970s, the continued existence of institutions such as the SONACOTRA and the re-employment of army veterans and civil servants who had worked in Algeria, allowed many colonial routines and ideas to keep on informing French public policies of accommodation of North African immigrants and Muslim practices.

For historical reasons, there existed powerful mechanism of diffusion that allowed the colonial legacy to continue shaping French public policies in the post-war period. One of the most important mechanisms thereby was the continued existence of the Paris Mosque, which developed from begin a symbol of loyalist Islam in the colonial era into an institution seen as the privileged partner for successive French governments to create an 'Islam of France'. Among the more stable strategies of governance was the constant distinction between 'good' and 'bad' Islam. In the colonial era the French positively evaluated an Islam that was only a religious belief and an Islam that was 'syncretized' in nature, as they believed to be the case with African Islam. The sponsorship of 'good Islam' resulted in attempts to co-opt Muslim leaders who were willing to support French rule and sporadically in the financing of institutions such as mosques, Madrasas and imams. Far more recently, since the 1980s, 'good Islam' came to be associated with particular ways of manifesting Muslim religious identity and practice. Thereby degrees of religious observance and whether or not Muslims abstained from wearing the headscarf, whether or not they visited the mosque or observed the Ramadan came to be seen as indicative of their level of 'integration' (cf. also Bowen, 2009, p. 128). At the level of Islamic organizations the formation of ethnic institutions and larger Islamic centers was seen as illustrative of 'fundamentalism', 'communalism' and the creation of 'parallel societies' that risked undermining the Republican model. The Paris Mosque, on the other hand, was believed to exemplify what an 'Islam of France' would be like. Again, strategies of financial support, selective collaboration and official state recognition were used to support this 'good Islam'.

In the first decade of the 21st century, French governing strategies have become more diversified. In the domain of Islamic organizations and representative institutions, governance is strongly grounded in Gallican and Concordatarian traditions, which is demonstrated by the ways the state has orchestrated, and continues to orchestrate, the functioning of the French Council of the Muslim Religion. In the domain of public education and with regard to the regulation of religious symbolism in the public realm more generally, the multi-interpretable concept of *laïcité* continues to legitimize efforts to impose the Republican model and disallow Islamic symbols, including the headscarf. However, with regard to facilities and institutions that are seen as catering to basic religious needs, a considerable effort has been made to improve the opportunities for Islam. The idea that a new form of 'vicinity Islam' is emerging and the hope that a ‘serene’ form of Islamic practice is coming into existence has legitimized efforts to improve the situation of Muslim cemeteries, mosques, places for ritual slaughtering and other kinds of facilities. Simultaneously, Muslim communities in France thereby obtain new opportunities to develop a religious infrastructure that is no longer under the tutelage of French public authorities.

## References

Achi, R. (2004). La séparation des Églises et de l'État à l’épreuve de la situation coloniale: L’État colonial et l’usage politique de la dérogation dans l’administration du culte musulman en Algérie (1907-1959). *Politix, 17*(66), 81-106.

Achi, R. (2005). La laïcité en situation coloniale: Usages politiques croisés du principe de séparation des Églises et de l’État en Algérie. In F. Banat-Berger (ed.), *La justice en Algérie (1830-1962)* (pp. 163-176). Paris: La Documentation Française.

Bayoumi, M. (2000). Shadows and light: Colonial modernity and the Grande Mosquée of Paris. *The Yale Journal of Criticism, 13*(2), 267-292.

Blanchard, P., Bancel, N. et al. (eds.). (2005). *La fracture coloniale: La société française au prisme de l’héritage colonial.* Paris: Editions la Découverte.

Bowen, J.R. (2006). *Why the French don’t like headscarves: Islam, the state and public space.* Princeton and Oxford: Princeton University Press.

Bowen, J.R. (2007). A view from France on the internal complexity of national models. *Journal of Ethnic and Migration Studies, 33*(6), 1003-1016.

Bowen, J.R. (2009). Schémas fonctionnels et modèles normatifs dans la politique française en matière d’islam. *Migrations Société, 21*(122), 107-136.

Bozzo, A. (2006). Islam et citoyenneté en Algérie sous la Troisième République: Logiques d’émancipation et contradictions coloniales (l’exemple des lois de 1901 et 1905). In P.-J. Luizard (ed.), *Le choc colonial et l'islam* (pp. 197-222). Paris, La Découverte.

Brubaker, R. (1992). *Citizenship and nationhood in France and Germany.* Cambridge: Harvard University Press.

Cohen, M. (2009). Jews and Muslims in France: Changing responses to cultural and religious diversity. In R. Grillo et al. (eds.), *Legal practice and cultural diversity* (pp. 219-236). Burlington: Ashgate.

Cross, G.S. (1983). *Immigrant workers in industrial France: The making of a new laboring class*. Philadelphia: Temple University Press.

Cruise-O'Brien, D. (1967). Toward an 'Islamic policy' in French West Africa 1854-1914. *Journal of African History, 8*(2), 303-316.

De Galembert, C. (2005). The city's 'nod of approval' for the Mantes-la-Jolie mosque project: Mistaken traces of recognition. *Journal of Ethnic and Migration Studies, 31*(6), 1141-1159.

Favell, A. (1998). *Philosophies of integration: Immigration and the idea of citizenship in France and Britain*. Hampshire: Palgrave.

Frégosi, F. (et al.). (2006). *L'Exercice du culte musulman en France: Lieux de prière et d'inhumation*. Paris: La documentation française.

Geisser, V. & Zemouri, A. (2007). *Marianne et Allah: Les politiques français face à la 'question Musulmane'*. Paris: La Découverte.

Ginésy-Galano, M. (1984). *Les immigrés hors la cité: Le système d'encadrement dans les foyers 1973-1982*. Paris: L'Harmattan.

Harrison, C. (1988). *France and Islam in West Africa, 1860-1960*. Cambridge: Cambridge University Press.

Jansen, Y. (2006). *Stuck in a revolving door: Secularism, assimilation and democratic pluralism*. Amsterdam: PhD University of Amsterdam.

Kepel, G. (1991). *Les banlieues de l'Islam: Naissance d'une religion en France*. Paris: Éditions du Seuil.

Kepel, G. (1994). *A L'Ouest d'Allah*. Paris: Editions du Seuil.

Le Pautremat, P. (2003). *La politique musulmane de la France au Xxe siècle: De l'Hexagone aux terres d'islam: espoirs, réussites, échecs*. Paris: Maisonneuve & Larose.

Lorcin, P.M. (1995). *Imperial identities: Stereotyping, prejudice and race in colonial Algeria*. London and New York: I.B. Tauris Publishers.

Machelon, J.P. (2006). *Rapport de la commission Machelon sur la laïcité*. Paris: La Documentation Française.

MacMaster, N. (1997). *Colonial migrants and racism: Algerians in France, 1900-1962*. London/New York: MacMillan Press.

MacMaster, N. (2002). Imperial façades: Muslim institutions and propaganda in inter-war Paris. In T. Chafer & A. Sackur (eds.), *Promoting the colonial idea: Propaganda and visions of empire in France* (pp. 71-81). New York, Palgrave.

Maurer, S. (2006). *Muslim worship in France: Practical stakes and response of public actors*. Paris: ICMEC.

Maussen, M. (2007, June 16). *The governance of Islam in Western Europe: A state of the art*. IMISCOE working paper, Amsterdam.

Maussen, M. (2009). *Constructing mosques: The governance of Islam in France and the Netherlands*. Amsterdam: PhD University of Amsterdam.

Noriel, G. (1988). *Le creuset français: Histoire de l'immigration XIX-XX siècle*. Paris: Éditions du Seuil.

Rosenberg, C. (2006). *Policing Paris: The origins of modern immigration control between the Wars*. Ithaca: Cornell University Press.

Safran, W. (2003). Pluralism and multiculturalism in France: Post-Jacobin transformations. *Political Science Quarterly, 118*(3), 437-465.

Shepard, T. (2006). *The invention of decolonization: The Algerian war and the remaking of France*. Ithaca: Cornell University Press.

Stora, B. (1992). *Ils venaient d'Algérie: L'immigration algérienne en France (1912-1992)*. Paris: Fayard.

Weil, P. (2004). *La France et ses étrangers: L'aventure d'une politique de l'immigration de 1936 à nos jours*. Paris: Gallimard.

# Globalization, the nation-state and religious newcomers

## Reflections on two countries

James Kennedy

Religion has not made a comeback in Western Europe. There continues to be a decline in practice and adherence, also in countries like France and the Netherlands, where church membership has, by European standards, been low since the mid-20th century. Migration from more religiously active parts of the globe has partially softended this trend. The transformation of religion into forms of individual spirituality is an important development, but the effects of this kind of spirituality on public and private life is hard to gauge. It may then be wrong to assume that religion will be eviscerated from Europe, but to speak of its resurgence is equally erroneous (see for the Netherlands the discussion between Kennedy, 2005 and Van Harskamp, 2005).

What has happened, however, is that the place of religion in respect to state and society has 'returned' as an important source of public debate. To what extent religious conscience, religious groups and religious organizations should be accommodated (or restricted) is now a concern that increasingly has drawn attention and often strongly divergent points of view. The headdress of Islamic women is the most emblematic issue of this trend, but it is hardly the only one. The question of how to order religion has turned out to be an issue even in societies where religion, at least for most, plays a pretty marginal role.

There are various factors that account for this attention to religion. In the first place, the very decline of religious practice has generated calls to rearrange the relationship between religious organizations and the state. In the Netherlands, for example, the growing debate over whether to subsidize (orthodox) religious schools has been possible by the very fact that much of the public no longer sees much need for a (strict) religious education. Secularization, one could say, made this debate possible. Similarly, the refusals of some priests in the Netherlands to deny the sacrament to openly gay parishioners prompted calls for a government crackdown on such forms of 'discrimination'. While such calls are unlikely, at least for now, to be honored, the room for religious groups to hold moral points of view at variance with predominant sensibilities has proven to be one of the most important sources of the debate over the place of religion in society. And though these debates may partly be informed by a desire to head off future 'Islamization', they are also made possible precisely by the shift from a society with more explicit religious underpinnings to one where religious influence is much more attenuated.

But if secularization paradoxically accounts for a new need to redefine religion in the public sphere, there is a second factor at work that accounts for a new interest in religion: the social utility of religion for public life. With the decline of the welfare state, the state increasingly has had to rely on civil society and the active participation of citizens. Interest in religious organizations has been revived in part because of its potential for increasing social cohesion and citizen activism. After all, religious movements, in 'deprivatizing' religious convictions, have been highly successful participants in some countries, as José Casanova (1994) pointed out fifteen years ago. And even in countries where such mass movements are absent, religious organizations, Sophie van Bijsterveld (2008) has argued, are likely to play an increasingly significant role as partners with government and other agencies of civil society. The rediscovered value of religion as a 'civic resource' has also meant that not only government but also religious organizations have had to rethink the place of religion in their respective societies (Kennedy, 2009). But this new appreciation for the utility of religion is not uncontested, and here, too, the debate can be sharp, as evidenced in the American discussion over government partnership with 'faith-based initiatives'.

Finally, debate over the place of religion in state and society has been intensified by globalization, in particular the presence of those who constitute the theme of this book, the 'religious newcomers'. Countries like France and the Netherlands have not become more religious, but they have become more religiously diverse, and it is this growing pluralism that has fed much of the new discussion over the place of religion. Obviously this discussion, at least in countries like the Netherlands and France, has often focused on Islam. And much of the discussion has had to do with the role of the state, and in which ways the state can, and should remain neutral. In the Netherlands, there are those who argue, for example, that the state cannot be neutral toward non-violent but deeply 'isolationist' Islamic groups whose presence is a threat to the health of Dutch democracy (Dercon, 2009). Anti-Islamic politics is manifest in various European countries, with the freedom of expression (often defined as the right to offend) commonly pitted against the freedom of religion (the right of religious newcomers not to feel offended).

These are broad transnational patterns, evident in Sweden or Spain as much as they are in France or the Netherlands. Yet the national context matters, because the nation-state still – at least to a large extent – continues to define how religion may legitimately be ordered. They are not the only actors who matter, but national experience remains crucial. Turkish-Muslim Germans who want to set up an organization will emphasize its religious character to receive state subsidies, while Turkish-Muslim Dutch citizens will emphasize the cultural purposes of their envisaged organization in order to receive government subsidies (Kortmann, 2009). A systematic effort to compare national experiences and practices is then very much worth the while.

To be sure, comparing nation states is a risky intellectual undertaking. There is an abiding danger that the differences between the two will be overemphasized, serving to confirm the well-established differences between the two countries. Or alternately it may, in conceiving of nation-states as hermetically sealed entities, too easily ignore transnational realities, in which nations are themselves part and parcel of wider patterns of transmission and mutual influence.

Yet the editors of this volume have rightly attempted to contribute to such an endeavor, and the collective result is an important analysis of how two European countries, France and the Netherlands, have accommodated religious newcomers and religious minorities. The starting point is, in fact, the difference between the two nations, arguing that the interaction between religion, nation and 'civil culture' (defined here as a 'national narrative') generated 'diverging reactions' to Islam in France and the Netherlands, as Thijl Sunier argues in his introduction to this volume. And as several contributions in this book make clear, this divergence between the Dutch and French contexts has not been restricted to the recent debate over Islam, but has extended back over time. Both the Netherlands and France, like other nation-states, have long been 'active agents' in 'domesticating' religion for their own purposes, as Sunier further notes. But the 'modes of civil incorporation' differed in the two countries, as did the terms under which religious minorities could expect to be 'integrated'.

But if the emphasis in the book is on difference, Sunier's emphasis on the importance of 'national discourses' and 'disparate civil cultures' in accounting for differing French and Dutch approaches to religion in the public sphere does not assume these cultures to be fixed or unchanging – or that national states were the only actors that counted. On the contrary, the religious subjects of national policies and pressures themselves helped to determine sometimes unpredictable outcomes. Neither the national state nor the various minorities discussed in this volume wholly dictated the terms of a shifting religious *modus vivendi*. Rather, it was the interaction between them that proved decisive, as Bérengère Massignon argues in her chapter on French *laïcité*. Such interactions resulted in quite different outcomes: not only 'national conflict' but 'local compromises' were crucial to how French schools and Islamic students reached a modus Vivendi. Nor was the state the only actor. And as Erik Sengers has stressed in his contribution, it was not only, or even primarily, the historically Protestant elites who in the Netherlands oversaw the integration of Roman Catholics, but Catholics themselves who played an important role in claiming their own public space. National states might seek to 'domesticate' religion, but at the same time it seems that, if Sengers' thesis can be more broadly applied, that religious-minded citizens largely domesticated themselves. The differences outlined here were not only the creation of two rather different states.

If this volume, then, continues to distinguish Dutch patterns of dealing with religion in the public sphere, (consociational, pragmatic or pluralist) from French patterns (republican, universalist or laicist), the contributors at the same time challenge the notion that such patterns are immutably ingrained in the political traditions of the respective nation states. They show that while the current Dutch and French approaches to managing religious pluralism have remained distinct from each other, these approaches have been anything but stable, changing as they have substantially, perhaps even radically, over time. Furthermore, several contributions show that the range of possibilities within the respective national discourses and political cultures are polyvalent enough to defy predetermined outcomes. And they show that beyond the difference in professed political principles the Dutch and French approach to organizing religious diversity sometimes show striking parallels, whether in the pragmatic concessions to a difficult-to-manage religious reality, or in the ordering of religions on the basis of implicit hierarchies.

The value of this book thus lies in the creative tension between on the one hand, a further analysis of the differences between the French and the Dutch cases, and on the other, a critical examination of all-too-facile claims about ostensibly salient, historically-grounded differences between France and the Netherlands.

## Change and continuity

The critical examination pertains to the time frame in which national difference arose. Both Wayne Te Brake and Peter Van Rooden challenge the assumption that it is the modern nation-state of the last two centuries which defined a persisting political culture in which religion was fit into a permanent national mould. Each, however, articulate radically different interpretations in doing so. For Te Brake, a better historical view is afforded by eliminating the false dichotomy that has improperly separated the early modern world from the modern. He sees Dutch consociationalism stemming from an older Dutch republicanism, just as the 'universalist' French mode of recent times has been shaped by seventeenth and eighteenth-century absolutism. Seen this way, distinct national patterns in respect to religion is not determined by modern processes of democratization or state formation, but by much older patterns of dealing with religious challenges. Van Rooden does not deny the existence of historical patterns per se; he concedes that religion, because it has loomed large in Dutch history, has always mattered in the process of Dutch state formation. Yet the ways in which the Dutch negotiated religion has changed so much in the course of the last centuries that historians can only fruitfully speak of 'radical discontinuity'. For Te Brake, we need to go back to the sixteenth century to understand current Dutch and French efforts to come to terms with Islam; for Van Rooden, it is not useful to go much further back than the 1960s, when the Netherlands rather rapidly broke with its pillarized structures. A post-Christian Netherlands has chosen to negotiate with Islam in a very different way than the same country would have half a century ago, Van Rooden claims. He would contest the idea that current Dutch practice in respect to Islam can have much to do with pillarization.

The study of history is about determining a proper balance between continuities and discontinuities, and this book has tried to find a balance between recognizing persistent patterns which continue, over time, to define the accommodation of religion and nation and recognizing contingency and the constantly shifting historical conditions which inarguably alter the conditions of the relationship. What the contributors help illustrate is that national political discourses and civil cultures did help create identifiable long-term parameters for the ways in which religion is, and is not, configured in public life. Not only French colonial policies, established in the nineteenth century, have continued to exercise an influence on how the French government acts toward Islam and toward

Muslims, as Marcel Maussen shows in his chapter, but also the 'Concordatarian traditions' of the Napoleonic period, with roots, arguably, in the sixteenth century. It seems clear enough that both the Dutch have drawn from past arrangements in ordering their religious lives – Dutch Muslims, for example, can continue to create their own institutions along much the same lines that Christian organizations that preceded them could, even if their willingness to do so is less, and even if public support for such institutions has become more problematic. It is moreover evident that many Dutch and French continue to appeal to particular national traditions, such as the French do with *laïcité*, that these appeals are rooted in historically shared experience, and that these ideas and practices help account for the fact that over long periods of time the French and the Dutch have accommodated religion in ways that continue to differ, in more or less the same way, from each other.

But it must be said at the same time that the parameters of national discourse are wide, allowing for multiple interpretations that change, sometimes very substantially, over time. Several chapters make clear that even within the span of a few years, supposedly stable political concepts are subject to reinterpretation and permutation. As Sunier has noted in his chapter on Islam in the Netherlands, competing liberal and communal traditions that for years vied with each other in defining the ways in which (religious) migrants integrated into society have themselves in recent years each split into differing camps, with each camp generating new factions that alternately demand a hardline and more accommodating stance toward religious newcomers.

Sunier's introduction to this book can serve as the basis for making a broader point: that national discourses are seldom if ever at any point univocal, and that they are usually contested and subjected to redefinition. Secular republicanism, so apparently foundational to France's political order, was opposed by a very significant part of the French population throughout the nineteenth and much of the twentieth centuries. Furthermore, France was never as rigorously laicist as some might suppose; the French state sometimes made common cause with the Catholic Church, and after the 1950s it partially financed religious education. In parallel fashion, Dutch pillarization, purportedly so characteristically Dutch, was resisted even in its heyday by many secularists and Protestants who thought that it detracted from the social unity they thought the Netherlands required. In short, the recognition of long-term discursive patterns in the civil culture of a nation must be accompanied by the recognition that dissonances and conflicts that exist within national political traditions repeatedly shift the terms under which religion is accorded a place in society.

## The cultural stance of religious minorities crucial

Another major set of variables in the shifting terms in which religion is nationally accommodated are the strategies developed by religious minorities themselves. That is one of the major premises of this book, and it is most thoroughly worked out in the contribution of editor Erik Sengers in his contribution. As briefly noted above, the shifting stance of Dutch Roman Catholics was the most crucial element in their own long-term accommodation within the wider Dutch society. Indeed, Sengers goes so far as to say that 'the general framework of the modern, liberal, pluralistic and national Dutch state remained stable in the modern period'. Rather, he argues, it was the Church that shifted its orientation, alternating between an initially more cooperative stance with the state, to greater antipathy later in the nineteenth century, then back to a more engaged stance which eventually resulted, in the decades after the Second World War, in the 'assimilation' of Dutch Catholics, in which the organizations that defined their separated religious identity 'disintegrated'. Whether the Dutch state really did retain the same stance throughout the nineteenth and twentieth centuries has been questioned by Van Rooden and his emphasis on discontinuity, but Sengers' salient point is that minorities like the Dutch Catholics are not merely the subjects of national policy, but are active, even decisive actors in the outcome.

Of course, it matters what kind of minorities we are talking about. For most of the twentieth century, Dutch Roman Catholics constituted some 40% of the national population, and were a strongly cohesive group, forming in the years after the First World War a power bloc of the first order. With their political party good for up to a third of the total vote, Roman Catholics could not be sidelined. In this respect, they differed sharply from the other Christian minority covered in this book, the French Protestants. At a mere 2% of the population, they could not aspire to the level of influence ultimately attained by Dutch Catholics. At the same time, however, their history of a minority was not the history of social emancipation as was the case for Dutch Catholics, who in general terms lagged behind Protestants in education, status and income. French Protestants were socially well-positioned, and its members were often enthusiastic contributors to France's five republics, several of them playing crucial roles in French public life. That may be changing now, as French Protestants now consist to an important degree of immigrant groups with less established access to political power and social influence. And French Protestants were always more fragmented than Dutch Catholics once were, a characteristic they share with a fissiparous Islam in Holland and France, however monolithic it may seem to the public eye. Not all minorities are the same; size and status are all factors that determine to what extent, and in which ways, minority religious groups assert themselves, and to what extent they are accorded a place in society.

Indeed, the size of minorities do arguably matter in France and the Netherlands, the two countries with the highest percentages of Muslims in Western Europe, where the fear of 'islamization' of Europe is driven in part by the high concentrations of Muslims in some of the larger Dutch and French cities. The educational levels and socio-economic status of immigrants also matter; American Muslims enjoy nearly the same level of income as other Americans do, removing one source of tension between Muslims and non-Muslims. The place that Islamic minorities can claim for themselves in part, too, will depend on having educational opportunities and seizing upon them.

## The persistent role of the state

But none of this means that in some facile way all tensions will dissipate if Muslims quickly assimilate and lift themselves up by their bootstraps. The very debate over which concessions schools should grant to Muslims in general and Muslim women in particular (with headdress as the emblematic issue) is an indication that the path to 'emancipation' or 'integration' is, perhaps inevitably, charged with tensions and conflict. These cannot be easily removed. As Massignon argues in this volume, there is an 'implicit hierarchies of religions' in France, which categorizes religions on the basis of longstanding presence, level of integration, degree of notoriety and the level of danger they represent. The same is true in the Netherlands, where – even now – there is residual public prejudice against Roman Catholics, consonant with a longer sense of the Netherlands as a Protestant nation. Public perceptions in both the Netherlands and France regard Muslims by definition as less integrated than, say, Buddhists or Hindus, regardless of the fact that their language skills or contacts with citizens beyond their own group belie such assumptions. Secular states do not treat all religious minorities equally, not only because the designation 'religious minority' covers an extremely wide range of groups, but also because state and society clearly find it more important to monitor – and regulate – specific religions that are regarded as more problematic than others.

To perceive the shared sense of hierarchy that disadvantages both Dutch and French Muslims is not to argue that the Netherlands and France have shown, either in the long-term or in recent decades, the same patterns in accommodating and regulating religious minorities. Scientology, to cite a particularly controversial example of a new religious 'cult', was able to start operations in the Netherlands with little difficulty (a government report in the early 1980s successfully advised the government to leave new religious groups alone), a very difficult situation than their fate in France. Up to present day, Dutch houses of worship are less regulated than in France, as religious groups do not need to register with the government. The Dutch state did not regulate its relations with the papacy via concordat (although it briefly attempted to do so in the 1820s), and the Dutch colonial government's serious efforts to regulate Islam in Indonesia was not as self-evidently applied to the Netherlands' new Muslim residents, who largely came from countries outside the former colonial orbit, arriving in a country, furthermore, that was trying its best to forget its colonial past. That does not mean that the colonial past matters not at all in contemporary Holland, but that the links are more ambiguous, perhaps, than in France, where Islam continued to constitute a factor in French relations with its former colonies, and the immigrants that originated there.

But however much French and Dutch modes may continue to be distinct from each other, the question might be raised to what extent France and the Netherlands increasingly resemble each other in efforts to regulate, accommodate and 'domesticate' religion – and in the contours of public debate over the place of religion. It is not only that these countries have among the highest percentages of Muslims in Europe; both countries are within the most secularized part of the continent, with relatively low levels of church membership. In this largely unchurched region of Europe, it is at least plausible to argue that both a suspicion of, and unfamiliarity of religion, has made it easier for Islam to be easily 'foreignized', to link Van Rooden's argument with Sunier's. In statistical terms, France and the Netherlands are the two countries where one might expect a dominant secularism to conflict most with substantial Islamic minorities.

But this is not what I chiefly mean when discussing the possibility of the Dutch and French traditions converging with each other. It is rather that both countries are divided over the place of religion in public life, and uncertain what kind of role the various religions could play, and should play. Many Dutch have recently been drawn to French *laïcité* as the way to achieve a thorough 'separation of church and state', itself a concept only recently in vogue in the Netherlands. To achieve this separation, they are willing to put an end to Holland's pillarized system of education, which still gives schools wide latitude to determine their own religious identity, at taxpayer expense. In this, they have found common cause with French laicists, who believe that religious practice must be separated from public life. At the same time, there are countervailing voices in France, the Netherlands and Europe that would encourage, for a variety of pragmatic and principled considerations, the (continued) inclusion of 'positive' forms of religious expression in the public sphere. In France there is a trend, with president Sarkozy's positive utterances over the need for religion in public life as example, that has expressed its openness to the role of religion in national life. Efforts to stimulate a 'neighborhood Islam' in France parallel efforts in the Netherlands and elsewhere to stimulate a religious institutions to act as civic resources on the local level, becoming integral parts of civil society. Such efforts need not necessarily be seen as disinterested or benevolent, but is sometimes advanced out of considerations that see religion as 'useful' to society, or alternately, that seek – particularly with Islam in mind – to 'domesticate' religion.

## A provisional conclusion

None of these impulses is entirely new and, as this volume shows, the various efforts to domesticate, accommodate or marginalize religion are recurring patterns in French and Dutch history. But for all the ways in which their national pasts continue to shape the ways in which the Dutch and the French respectively grapple with religion, both countries are confronted, I think, with truly new, and similar, challenges. Like many other Europeans, the Dutch and the French are clearly confronted with rethinking the place of religion in societies that once had thought religion wholly irrelevant. They furthermore need to come to more balanced terms with a religion – Islam – which Europeans, I think, wish 'foreignized' *and* 'domesticated', almost in the same breath. And last but not least, Europeans belonging to religious minorities – Protestant and Catholic, Christian and Muslim, and the many other groups not examined in this volume – need to reimagine the place of their own religious traditions in a landscape that for them is, just as much as it is to their secular neighbors, *terra incognita.*

## References


Casanova, J. (1994). *Public religions in the modern world.* Chicago-London: University of Chicago Press.

Dercon, P. (2009). Bescherming van de democratische rechtsorde en vrijheid van godsdienst. In A.J. Nieuwenhuis & C.M. Zoethout (eds.), *Rechtsstaat en religie: Staatsrechtconferentie 2008, Universiteit van Amsterdam* (pp. 201-211). Nijmegen: Wolf Legal Publishers.

Kennedy, J.C. (2005) Recent Dutch religious history and the limits of secularization. In E. Sengers (ed.), *The Dutch and their gods: Secularization and transformation of religion in the Netherlands since 1950* (pp. 27-42). Hilversum: Verloren.

Kennedy, J.C. (2009). Die niederländischen protestantischen Kirchen auf der Suche nach einer öffentlichen Rolle. In A. Bauerkämper & J. Nautz (eds.), *Zwischen Fürsorge und Seelsorge: Christliche Kirchen in den europäischen Zivilgesellschaften seit dem 18. Jahrhundert* (pp. 259-285). Frankfurt am Main: Campus.

Kortmann, M. (2009, september). *Religionsgemeinschaft versus sozial-kulturelle Organisation: Das Selbstverständnis islamischer Organisationen in Deutschland und den Niederlanden.* Paper presented at the meeting of the Deutsche Vereinigung für Politische Wissenschaft DVPW, Kiel.

Van Bijsterveld, S. (2008). *Overheid en godsdienst: Herijking van een onderlinge relatie.* Nijmegen: Wolf Legal Publishers.

Van Harskamp, A. (2005). Simply astounding: Ongoing secularization in the Netherlands? In E. Sengers (ed.), *The Dutch and their gods: Secularization and transformation of religion in the Netherlands since 1950* (pp. 43-57). Hilversum: Verloren.

**About the authors**

James C. Kennedy is historian and professor of Dutch history since the Middle Ages at the Universiteit van Amsterdam. He has written several books on political and cultural developments in Dutch postwar history, and has published extensively on the Dutch religious past, including a recent book on the history of Dutch Protestant churches since 1848.

Bérengère Massignon graduated at Sciences Po (Paris) and recieved her PhD in sociology from the Ecole Pratique des Hautes Etudes (EPHE). She is a researcher with the GSRL (Groupe Sociétés, Religions et Laïcités), a joint research unit between the CNRS and the EPHE. She teaches geopolitics of religion and sociology. Her research is focused on the European Union and religions. She has published a.o. *Gods and bureaucrats: Religions and secularisms facing the challenges of European integration* (Rennes, 2007) and - co-authored with Virginie Riva - *God in changing in Europe: Heritages and new challenges* (Paris, 2010).

Marcel Maussen is an Assistant Professor at the department of Political Science of the University of Amsterdam and affiliated with the Institute for Migration and Ethnic Studies (IMES) and the Amsterdam Institute for Social Science Research (AISSR). He studied political science and philosophy in Amsterdam, Aix-en-Provence and Paris. In 2009 he obtained his PhD degree (with honor) for a dissertation entitled *Constructing mosques. The governance of Islam in France and the Netherlands*. His research interests include the governance of religious and cultural pluralism, political theory, comparative institutionalism and Islam in Europe.

Peter van Rooden obtained his Ph.D. (cum laude) in 1985 at Leiden University with a study on biblical criticism in 17th century Leiden (*Theology, biblical scholarship and rabbinical studies in the seventeenth century: Constantijn L' Empereur (1591-1648), Professor of Hebrew and Theology at Leiden*, Leiden, Brill 1989). In 1996 he published a study of the radical changes in the relation between religion, society, and political power in the Netherlands since the sixteenth century: *Religieuze Regimes. Over godsdienst en maatschappij in Nederland, 1570-1999* (Amsterdam: Bert Bakker). During the academic year 1997/98 he was a visiting professor at the History Department of the University of Michigan, Ann Arbor. He is currently working on a book about the radical dechristianisation which took place in the Netherlands since the 1960s, based on oral history.

Erik Sengers studied sociology and theology in Amsterdam (VU and UvA), Hamburg, and Utrecht and earned his PhD at the Catholic Theological University (Utrecht) with a dissertation on the history of Dutch Catholicism since 1795 from rational-choice perspective. He specialised in mainline churches in the Netherlands and Europe, religious markets and religious marketing, and religion in modern society. His current research is about mainline churches in global society. He is assistant-professor at the Faculty of Social Sciences (department sociology) of VU University (Amsterdam).

Thijl Sunier (1954), anthropologist, holds the VISOR chair of 'Islam in European Societies' at VU University (Amsterdam). He conducted research on inter-ethnic relations, Turkish youth and Turkish Islamic organisations in the Netherlands, comparative research among Turkish youth in France, Germany, Great Britain and the Netherlands, and international comparative research on nation building and multiculturalism in France and The Netherlands. Presently he is preparing research on styles of popular religiosity among young Muslims in Europe, religious leadership, and nation-building and Islam in Europe. He is member of the Amsterdam School for Social Science Research (ASSR), chairman of the board of the Inter-academic School for Islam Studies in the Netherlands (ISIS). He is editor of the anthropological journal *Etnofoor*, and chairman of the board of the Dutch Anthropological Association (ABV).

Wayne te Brake is Professor of European History at Purchase College in the State University of New York. A graduate of the University of Michigan, he has written broadly on the themes of revolution, contentious politics and religious co-existence in early modern Europe. The research presented in this essay was supported by project grants from the Ford Foundation. Professor te Brake is the author of *Regents and rebels: The revolutionary world of an eighteenth century Dutch city* (1989) and *Shaping history: Ordinary people in European politics, 1500-1700* (1998).

Jean-Paul Willaime is Research Director at l'*Ecole Pratique des Hautes Etudes*, Department of Religious Studies, Sorbonne, Paris. He is member of the *Group Societies, Religions, Laïcities* (GSRL, Research Centre EPHE-CNRS) and Director of the *European Institute of Religious Studies*. His fields of research are mainline and evangelical Protestantism, religions and school education, Europe and religions, sociology of religions: history and theories.